THE FINE COMPANION

D.C. DAKING
AND
THE *LOG OF THE 'FINE COMPANION'*
1914

1. The 'Fine Companions'
'D'   'Alec'   'P'

THE FINE COMPANION

The Journal of a Caravan Trip
from Oxford to Stratford-upon-Avon
in the summer of 1914

edited by

HILARY CLARE

The Elsie Jeanette Oxenham Society/
The Abbey Chronicle
2011

First published in Great Britain
By The Elsie Jeanette Oxenham Society/
The Abbey Chronicle 2011
32 Tadfield Road, Romsey, Hampshire. SO51 5AJ

Text of *The Log of the 'Fine Companion'*
© The English Folk Dance and Song Society
Editorial text © Hilary Clare 2011

ISBN 978-0-9567834-0-0

A CIP catalogue record for this book is available from the British
Library.

Printed in England by Hobbs the Printers Ltd.
Brunel Road, Totton, Hampshire. SO40 3WX

CONTENTS

LIST OF ILLUSTRATIONS

The photographs on the front and back covers are reproduced on pp.42 and 22 respectively.

The background photograph on the cover shows the view from Epwell crossroads, where the 'fine companions' rested on 31 July 1914.

Acknowledgements:

1,4,8,9: *The Log of the 'Fine Companion'* 2:. *The Oxford Journal*, 12 June 1912; 18. *the Banbury Guardian 23 July 1914* (both Oxfordshire County Council Photographic Archive) 3,,5,6, *The Red Triangle*, the journal of the YMCA (July 1918, ;Vol.4 No.9 May 1921,; Vol.7 No.10 October 1923) (Birmingham University Library),7 the Post family; 7,12,13,14,15,16,17, author.

ACKNOWLEDGEMENTS

My warmest thanks are due to Malcolm Taylor, the Librarian of the Vaughan Williams Memorial Library at Cecil Sharp House, and to his staff, for their very great help over the years, and for permission to reprint the *Log of the 'Fine Companion.'*

Thanks in equal measure must go to all the friends in the Elsie Jeanette Oxenham Society who have helped in the production of this work, especially Ruth Allen and Lorraine Toogood.

D.C. Daking's family kindly answered my enquiries and gave much help in the early stages of my research.

The late Lord Polwarth, nephew, and Miss Bridget Capron, niece, of Alec Hepburne-Scott, kindly allowed me to photocopy Alec's privately-printed letters and quote from them in this work.

All quotations from the works of Elsie J. Oxenham are by kind permission of Elspeth Wendy Dunkerley and the estate of Elsie J. Oxenham.

Staff at the Surrey History Centre were helpful beyond the call of duty in assisting me with the Electoral Registers of Abinger Hammer.

Benedicta Ward and Joy Wotton answered questions. My long-suffering husband patiently accompanied me on photographic trips round Oxfordshire and has borne for over twenty years with my obsession with the *Log of the 'Fine Companion'*.

Hilary Clare

NOTES

Notes for editorial material and for the Appendices may be found at the end of each section.

Notes for the *Log of the 'Fine Companion'* are given as footnotes.

Dedicated
to the beloved memory
of my mother,
MARIE HELEN ISOBEL
WRIGHT, NÉE REID,
(1919-2009)
who first introduced me
to Elsie Jeanette Oxenham
and
'the Pixie'.

INTRODUCTION

DAISY Caroline Daking is nowadays much better known by the nickname 'the Pixie', invariably used by the girls' author Elsie Jeanette Oxenham when she depicted her in several of her 'Abbey' stories as an experienced and charismatic folk-dance teacher and as a wise friend and counsellor. The first of Oxenham's books to include 'the Pixie', *The Abbey Girls go back to School* (1922), was dedicated jointly to Helen Kennedy North (who appears in the book as 'Madam') and D.C. Daking 'with thanks for all they have given to me'. Both are known to have taught Oxenham dancing and may have first done so at the summer school of the English Folk Dance Society[1] held at Cheltenham in the summer of 1920. In the course of this book the nickname 'the Pixie' is bestowed on D.C. Daking not by Oxenham but by yet another transparently disguised real character, Catherine Orde, who appears as 'Miss Newcastle'.

If the popularity of Oxenham's books ensured that D.C. Daking would be remembered, her real-life exploits certainly warranted it. She was among the first of Cecil Sharp's pupils at the very beginning of the folk-dance revival of the early twentieth century, and during and after the First World War, as we shall see, taught folk-dances to the troops behind the lines and, later, in the Army of Occupation. Her subsequent work under the auspices of the YMCA came to an end when the financial difficulties of the 1920s caused funding cut-backs, and the last decade or so of her life seems to have been spent developing an interest in Jungian psychology while she earned a living doing various domestic jobs. She was clearly an attractive and dynamic personality, and it is fitting that she should not be forgotten.

Her contemporaries would inevitably have known her as 'Miss Daking'. There is strong evidence that, although originally named Caroline Daisy, she preferred to reverse her forenames and was known to her family as 'Daisy'; it is possible that Oxenham and others really did call her 'Pixie'. This presents problems for a biographer, for to refer to her as 'the Pixie' seems to cast the real D.C. Daking into the shade, yet to insist on 'Daisy' may confuse Oxenham enthusiasts. To call her simply 'Daking', employing current critical usage, seems inappropriately formal. A compromise solution is to use simply her initials, DCD, except in childhood, when 'Daisy' seems more appropriate, leaving 'the Pixie' for use when it is clear that it is the fictional character (however close to reality) which is being dealt with.

Similarly, to refer throughout in full to the English Folk-Dance Society and the Young Men's Christian Association would be tiresome, so again these organisations are referred to as the EFDS and the YMCA.

THE LOG OF THE "FINE COMPANION"

In the Vaughan Williams Memorial Library in Cecil Sharp House, London, headquarters of the English Folk Dance and Song Society, is a stout quarto note-book, 9 by 7 inches in page size and half an inch thick. It has a now shabby black morocco cover, bordered with a narrow gold line, and the page edges are gilded. The endpapers are marbled; the front one bears a stationer's label:

> Mawson Swan & Morgan Ltd.
> High-Class Stationers & Printer
> NEWCASTLE-UPON-TYNE

Pencilled on the fly-leaf is '3/6' – three shillings and sixpence, an apparently derisory amount in modern currency of 17.5 p but if compared with the contemporary price of a cheap novel can be seen to be rather more expensive than the cheapest and so in modern terms the equivalent of at least £7.50. In other words, the note-book represents both a substantial financial outlay and an indication of the seriousness of its purchaser's purpose. It was not a cheap notebook meant for an ephemeral record but a comparatively expensive purchase designed to be a permanent record of happy holidays.

The first page is simply headed 'The Log of The Fine Companion 1914', and with the following 33 pages, written on one side only, forms a diary covering 23 July to 6 August, with a last entry dated 28 November. A few later pages have been used as a scrapbook for photographs, letters and articles, with the remainder of the book left blank.

The *Log of the 'Fine Companion'* was kept by Daisy Daking, who consistently refers to herself as 'D' and to her companions as 'P' and 'Alec'. It has been possible to identify both 'P' and 'Alec' and to expand what was already known of 'D', so that the *Log* is set in its context and can add its record to the account of the last days of the 'long Edwardian' summer.

Caravans were rather the 'in thing' of the moment. There can be few who are not familiar with Toad's 'canary-coloured cart' (*The Wind in the Willows*, 1908), and another book of more transient popularity was Elizabeth von Arnim's *The Caravaners* (1909), a humourous account of a holiday not much enjoyed by a group of upper-class English people and a Prussian officer. Both these tie in with the *Log* in their views of the horse-drawn vans, the unspoiled English countryside (with all its drawbacks) and the joys – or otherwise – of the simple life. Daisy Daking's van was clearly seen by spectators as a little unusual, but it was not unique.

The notebook remained in the possession of its author for many years, since the last letter it contains is dated 1 May 1940. Either shortly before her death, therefore, or soon afterwards, it was given to the Vaughan William Memorial Library at Cecil Sharp House, where it remains.

DAISY CAROLINE DAKING

DAISY Caroline Daking, 'D', the author of the *Log of the Fine Companion*, was born in Ipswich on 23 August 1884. Her birth certificate speaks of her as 'Caroline Daisy', although she seems to have been called simply 'Daisy' by her family and friends (she refers to herself in the Log as 'D') and generally appears in records as 'Daisy Caroline'. Caroline was evidently after her paternal grandmother and great-grandmother; Daisy must have been her parents' choice. They were Frederick (Fred) Daking, a solicitor's clerk, and Elizabeth (Bessie), née Ashby; they had married in 1881. Their first child, a little boy called after his father, died at a few months old, but Daisy was followed by a second daughter, Mary Olive (Molly), born on 28 June 1886.

The Daking family came from Suffolk, as did Fred's mother, Caroline Waller, and seem to have been modestly well-off. Both Fred's father and grandfather were millers at Raydon, and his Waller grandfather was a farmer at Boxford; his Waller grandmother did not die until 1892, when Daisy was six. Fred Daking had evidently had sufficient education to fit him to be a solicitor's clerk, and he seems to have been interested in scientific matters, including photography. His wife came of a family from the Derbyshire-Leicestershire border area; her father at the time of her birth was a farmer, but gave up or lost his farm around 1870 and became a commercial traveller, later a tramcar driver in London. Bessie Ashby before her marriage worked as a draper's assistant in a big establishment in Ipswich, probably making the move to Suffolk because her mother's brother was established there in the same line of business.

By the time Daisy was four and Molly two they had been orphaned. Fred Daking died on 2 April 1888 and Bessie on 21 June in the same year, both of T.B. The little girls were adopted by their father's step-sister and her husband, Emily and Edmund Arthur Maxwell, who had no children of their own. These are the couple 'the Pixie' referred to as 'Uncle' and 'Aunt', and the relationship was clearly one of virtual parenthood.

This is the more remarkable because there was no blood relationship. What had happened was that Fred Daking's mother, born Caroline Waller, had been widowed quite young and had remarried. Her second husband was Matthias Jackson, a widower with two children, one of whom was the Emily who married Edmund Arthur Maxwell. She was less than a year older than her step-brother Fred Daking and had married within a few months of Fred and Bessie. When the young Dakings died so tragically, it may have been only Emily who was in a position to take care of Daisy and Molly, for although Fred's mother, Emily's step-mother, was still alive she was in Lancashire with her second husband and the five children of their marriage, the youngest of whom was only four years older than Daisy. Emily, in Hertfordshire, with no children of her own and a husband who evidently accepted the situation, was the obvious person to take charge of Daisy and

Molly. Fred Daking's grandmother, although living nearby in Ipswich, may, in her mid-seventies, not have felt capable of taking on such young children, though they did continue to visit her from time to time.

Edmund Arthur Maxwell was at this time, and for some considerable years to come, a professional photographer. In 1881, just before his marriage, he had been living in Hadley Green; by 1891 he, his wife and their wards, were at 50 High Street, Barnet; by 1901 they had moved to The Braes, Wellhouse Lane, Chipping Barnet. Mr Maxwell then made a career change, and by 1911 was established as the librarian at the Hyde Institute in Barnet; as this opened in 1904 he may have been there from its beginning. He and his wife seem to have stayed there until the early 1920s, when it appears from the account given of them in Elsie Jeanette Oxenham's *Queen of the Abbey Girls* (1926) that they retired to a newly-built bungalow ('Barnetholm') at Abinger in Surrey, where 'the Pixie' settled her 'van'. Emily Maxwell died in 1934 and her husband very quickly remarried, dying himself in 1949.

Edmund Maxwell was described by DCD as 'a Darwinian and an agnostic', who removed his niece from Sunday school because he disapproved of the system of rewarding children for learning texts by giving them pictures. 'He said it was a wrong principle to teach religion by means of rewardings.'[2] DCD alleged that she had been brought up without religion, and doubted that she had even been christened, but she does seem to have been taken to church and was at least exposed to Christianity, for she remarks that 'all the girls at my school were confirmed', but again Uncle opposed it for her on the grounds that it was too serious a matter and must wait till she was adult; she never did take the step.

She was certainly sensitive to church music and atmosphere (she records a favourable reaction to the plainsong and incense of St Alban's Holborn, encountered in her twenties), and to the beauty of, for instance, Canterbury Cathedral; interestingly (in view of the Oxenham connection) she felt an affinity with the monastic experience. All this tied in with a recurring dream of her childhood, in which she was on a stone staircase in a great building, with music (plainsong) coming from far away; later she felt that she came to live her stairway, not merely dream it, and felt 'at home and friendly' with 'Leander or Benedict or Thomas Aquinas or Saint Francis' and had 'a feeling of actual personal communication with hidden singing monks.'[3]

This is all we know of her childhood and youth. Where and how she first learned to dance is unfortunately a mystery, but by the spring of 1911 and the date of the census (2 April), aged 26, she is to be found at 3 Elmbank Mansions, Barnes, with what could be a married school friend or may simply be a landlady who also happened to come from Barnet. She is described as 'independent', but this may simply be that she was by now occupied in learning to dance. If she had earlier had any training for another career we have no evidence of it; her background was too genteel for her to contemplate a future in domestic service, but there is no indication that she trained as a teacher or as a secretary, the most common careers open to girls of her station. It is worth noting that her sister worked, and so presumably trained, as a nurse; DCD would almost certainly have expected to have to support herself. Both sisters were advised not to marry because of their parents' health record; Molly did, and died in childbirth; Daisy did not, and in spite of her recorded protestations to the contrary[4] may have regretted it.

In the autumn term of 1911, when she was of the same Barnes address, she enrolled at the South-Western (later Chelsea) Polytechnic in what were advanced dance classes: Morris on Tuesdays between 6 and 7, followed by a 'Teaching Dancing Class' on the same evening between 7 and 8; on Wednesday there was a 'Morris Dancing Class for Teachers Certificate' between 6.30 and 7.30. The following term (when her address was altered to her Oxford one) she enrolled for Cecil Sharp's 'Experimental Morris' class on Tuesdays between 8 and 9 and another Morris class on Thursdays between 6.30 and 7.30. The Country Dance classes do not appear in her timetable, but it may be that she was in fact teaching them: membership of the 'Experimental Morris' class shows that by this stage she was well advanced, as of course does the certificate class. The Chelsea class records show that DCD paid £1-11-6 for the Michaelmas Term and £1-1-0 for the Lent Term, quite substantial sums; it seems more than probable that she had attended other classes elsewhere and came to Chelsea, by now the official 'School of Morris', to put on a final polish and get a teaching qualification. It is tempting to wonder whether she had been involved with Mary Neal's Espérance League, whose original instructor had been William Kimber himself, but there is no mention of her in their records and she is not quite of the right social background, neither grand enough to be a friend of Neal's nor working-class enough (and too old) to be one of the girls.

But wherever she had learned to dance, when she arrived in Oxford in January 1912 to teach classes there she was described as 'one of Mr. Sharp's trained pupils.'[5]

An eye-witness of the early days of the Oxford branch of the English Folk Dance Society described her as 'London born, deadly efficient, three-feet high, with classes so huge she had to mount a high chair to conduct them. Professors and biologists vied for her instruction; rowing blues sat on her doorstep enquiring whether their left foot back shuffle was really coming on.'[6] Another witness of this period called her 'a little genius of a lady whose zest amounted almost to fanaticism.'[7] All descriptions of her remark on her small height and her passionate enthusiasm. The most familiar of these is of course Elsie Jeanette Oxenham's, in *The Abbey Girls Go Back to School* (1922). Here is one of the book's characters (Cicely Hobart) telling another ('Miss Newcastle') about her first encounter:

> '... she's tiny, but very very neat; I'm dying to see her in a tunic! She's a lovely dancer, too. Fair hair – glasses – bright quick blue eyes –every bit as bossy as Madam, though she's such a dot; but in quite a different way.'[8]

We are immediately told of her nickname, 'the Pixie', and as such she is an important character in Oxenham's Abbey books of this period, *The Abbey Girls Go Back to School* (1922), *The New Abbey Girls* (1923), *The Abbey Girls Again* (1924), *The Abbey Girls*

DAISY CAROLINE DAKING

in Town (1925) and *Queen of the Abbey Girls* (1926);[9] thereafter she disappears completely and there has been much speculation as to why. It may be that she asked Oxenham not to feature her again, or that Oxenham had by then lost touch with her, or that there was some sort of rift, perhaps caused by 'the Pixie' feeling that Oxenham had violated her privacy. It may also be that DCD had moved away from the folk-dance circles with which Oxenham was also by this time less closely associated. We are never now likely to know, but meanwhile Oxenham's five books are an important source of information about her. They present her not merely as a lively folk-dance teacher but also as a purveyor of wise advice. Her work with the troops in the First World War, which we shall deal with below, is featured, and also her later work in the East End of London and elsewhere. The final book, *Queen of the Abbey Girls*, has a detailed description of a visit to the 'van', by then apparently settled in Surrey, which again we shall come to in due course.

But first – Oxford. She stayed there from January 1912 to the summer of 1914, lodging at 11 Woodstock Road and making many friends, particularly perhaps the Sidgwick family. Her first work seems to have been with the Oxford Teachers' Club, for by March 1912, when the inaugural meeting of the local branch of the EFDS took place, she had 87 members, of whom 18 were brave and skilled enough to provide a demonstration of Playford dances in the presence of not just the public but also of Cecil Sharp himself. She also seems to have taught Reg Tiddy of New College, one of the first demonstration morris side of the Society, who

11

2. Photographs from *The Oxford Journal,* 12 June 1912, showing the demonstration at Thame by the Oxford EFDS. DCD is featured in the top left picture.

danced a morris jig with 'Mr Wright of the London Society'; Wright was specifically described as the only dancer of the evening who had not been taught by her[10]. The demonstration included DCD herself, who danced 'Princess Royal' alone; evidently at this period she was willing to perform, although later Oxenham records her as refusing to do so:

> 'She did not approve of women dancing morris jigs before an audience, though she knew others did not share her opinion; to her, morris was a man's dance, and though she would teach it she would not dance in public.'[11]

Two months later, at a demonstration in Thame, she performed again, and a photograph survives (see photograph on p.12), showing her with handkerchiefs, sun-bonnet, and long plaits. As in all her surviving photographs she looks rather serious, and there is no visual record of her 'bright quick blue eyes' and evident liveliness of expression in conversation.

The years in Oxford were probably the happiest of her life, full of activity and success, friendship and dancing. February 1914 saw the first act of tragedy, when her sister Molly, who had trained as a nurse and married in 1913, died after giving birth to a baby. The infant's father, an American by birth but of English descent and upbringing, who had served in the Royal Army Medical Corps for three years, was recalled to the service in 1914 and served in it until 1919; he remarried in 1917 and emigrated to Canada in 1920. He seems to have disclaimed responsibility for his son. The full story is not known; but whatever happened, DCD was to a certain extent involved with her nephew, though she did not take care of him personally. In the summer of 1914 he was being fostered in Headington, and DCD was busy making garments for him. It is curious that there is no mention of grief for her sister in the *Log*, but it may be that it was intended to be a semi-public document in which private sorrow had no place. She evidently had no intention of 'taking on' little Richard, and probably would not have been able to do so, since her work required constant moving around and she had no permanent home.

By the summer of 1914 her caravan, 'The Fine Companion' (named after the folk dance), was sited on Boar's Hill, in the grounds of The Plain, a house recently built by Miss C.O.Stevens. As the Oxford branch of the EFDS was now well established, Cecil Sharp had asked DCD to go to the north-east, to teach in Northumberland and Durham, beginning in September. Perhaps the van was intended to act as a base wherever she happened to be, envisaging a future of moving around the country, but in the meantime its first recorded journey was to be from Oxford up to Stratford-on-Avon for the summer festival of the EFDS. The first entries in the *Log of the Fine Companion* show DCD making ready for the trip, with some of the van's painting still being done. As the logbook itself bears the label of a Newcastle-on-Tyne stationer she must already have been north to make preliminary arrangements; perhaps the first date in the log, 23 July, represents not the first time of sleeping in it but the beginning of the Stratford excursion; as she describes it as needing a clear-out it may in fact have been in commission for some time, perhaps even since the previous summer, when DCD is recorded as 'camping' in a caravan at the Stratford summer school.[12]

The *Log* must speak for itself. It does not so much as end as simply come to a stop, after a few words about the War, with the anguished cry 'Perhaps this is a Dream, & all before was true – or was <u>that</u> the Dream. They cannot both be true – at least not in the same year?' But they could be, and were.

When war was declared on 4 August 1914 Cecil Sharp decided to continue the summer school, but its atmosphere changed radically. Many of the young men left immediately to join up – several were already territorials – and the rest must have been considering what to do. Lois Vidal, who was there for the second fortnight, records

> 'So while the troops were passing through the harvest fields of France to their swift destruction, we were one with a semi-preoccupied group of English youths. Lads of promise one by one slipped away to be heard of later in one or other regiment of the line, in casualty lists, or encountered strangely altered in some provincial hospital town.
>
> And we danced – and for the mid-morn interval met in the large elementary schoolroom, sitting on the edge of the platform dangling our legs, ostensibly to sing folk songs to Cecil Sharp's piano accompaniment on the said platform, actually to read the *Times* account of the landing, and later of Mons and the first fierce casualty list.'[13]

The folk-dance world changed almost overnight, though DCD did fulfil her promised engagement in the north. Judging by the report from the Northumberland and Durham branch in 1915, she taught two classes of teachers in Newcastle, and three other classes are mentioned besides

demonstrations. One of her pupils is recorded[14] as saying "Well, you'd never know she was from the *South*",
the highest possible compliment; certainly 'Miss Newcastle' in *The Abbey Girls Go Back to School* (who
probably attended one of those first classes for teachers)
was 'green, yellow, blue, and dandy-gray-russet with
envy' when the Abbey girls (as presumably Oxenham in
real life, for the speech sounds like a quotation) get her
as their teacher at Cheltenham.

But she had been working hard for three years,
followed by the enormous stress of the outbreak of the
Great War. The shock of seeing the happy world of
folk-dancing disintegrate and the young men going off
to be killed, seem to have taken their toll, for DCD is
recorded as having a breakdown in 1915,[15] and must
have gone home to 'Uncle' and 'Aunt' to recuperate.
Once recovered she was looking for a way to help the
war effort; 'Uncle' had left his library in Barnet and
gone to work in a YMCA. hut in France. By a fortunate
coincidence Lois Vidal, whom DCD had met on Boar's
Hill, was also in France and working for the YMCA at
le Havre. Her autobiography, *Magpie: the story of a
nymph errant,* tells us how DCD got to France:

> Earlier in my time there [i.e. spring 1917] my chief
> had said to me one day,
> "What can we do to improve the Concert Parties? I
> am so tired of the 'End of a Perfect Day' and Dvorák's
> 'Humoresque', and I know the troops could do with the best
> we could give them. …. I thought furiously for a few mo-
> ments and then said, "What about folk dancing?"
> "I've never come across it actually? What is it?
> Sort of Merry England in England's green and pleasant
> land?"

"Exactly," I said. "And I know it would go down with the British Army. It's exercise, art, self-expression and jolly good fellowship – they'll be *doing* it, not having it chucked at them in lumps of indigestible sentimentality. And I know the person who could put it across, probably the only one existing who could do it."

"Well," he said, with his eyes lit, "fire ahead. We'll get his pass through at once."

"It's not a him, it's a her; a wee body with personality just sticking out of her and the spirit of old England alive in her. She used to teach folk dancing in Oxford, went to Newcastle in 1914, had a breakdown in 1915, and has now retired from Morris in the Dance and is wasting her genius looking after an old public librarian and his wife, uncle or something, she calls him."

"But *where*?" said the General Secretary, leaning forward eagerly.

"In Barnet," I said. "But why?"

"Because her uncle is one of my best hut leaders," he said, turning to the telephone.

"Has Mr. Maxwell gone back to Cinder City yet? No? Then ask him to come up to my office."

I had never seen him do anything with so much decision and dispatch.

In three minutes a world-important conference of three was in progress, and the net result was that Mr. Maxwell, a true, shrewd and unselfish little man, went back to Barnet to release his niece for service in his stead.

"I've always wanted to do it," he said, "but Daisy wouldn't hear of it. Said she would never be allowed to come, and couldn't do it if she did. I know better; she's a marvel, that's what she is."

She came, and with a verve and fearlessness and enthusiasm soon got the thing going.'[16]

DCD herself does not mention Lois Vidal in this connection, attributing the recommendation of folk-dancing to a certain Helen Tuckett of Bristol, then acting as driver to the YMCA Base Secretary, but no matter who was responsible it was DCD who had the success. She wrote three accounts of her work, one for the YMCA Journal *The Red Triangle*; (1918) the second a report for the EFDS (1919), and the third an article in *English Dance and Song* (1940) obviously based on the earlier pieces. The *Red Triangle* article, which is the longest but least known, is worth quoting in full:

"THE VERY BEST JOB IN FRANCE."

The English Folk Lore Society [sic] *has offered the services of qualified instructors to visit the camps and teach the men country dances. Miss Daking tells how this revival of an old-time recreation was welcomed by the men in France.*

I will tell you of our new branch of the Y.M.C.A. work in France. We teach folk dancing to the troops. That, you will say, is ridiculous. The Army is not in France for that kind of thing. Soldiers, anyway, wouldn't care to dance; and, besides, look at their boots! And, of course, you are right, but I will tell you what has happened.

A Y.M.C.A. secretary in charge of the work at a base in France thought there might be room for something different from the usual concert party work, something that would be more of a pastime, and perhaps a hobby for the men. Because, at a base, you have thousands of more or less permanent men, who need help far more than one would at first imagine. Men living in camps, perhaps by the docks, for the unloading of ships, and all the bakers making bread for the Army, and engineers and motor men, and people in the Post Office, and in every kind of work. Tired men they often are, for they are not fit, or they would not be there. And they live in camps, perhaps built on cinders, and per-haps quite grim to look at, and their work is in shifts day in and day out, and when they are free there is the town to go to, with nothing to do but walk the streets and go to the ca-fés, and nothing English except, of course, the Y.M.C.A.

DAISY CAROLINE DAKING

The secretary talked to some of his helpers. Couldn't something be started which would meet his need? Some friend suggested folk dancing. The men might like it. It is sound and simple, and they like good things; it is merry, and they need fun; it has good tunes, and they love music. The secretary thought that he would experiment, and, being told of a young woman who had had a fair amount of experience under the English Folk Dance Society, he invited her to come out and see what happened, and she arrived in France at the end of May, 1917.

It was a little difficult at first. No one seemed to know much about folk dances, and a good many people considered the whole thing to be somewhat silly. Folk wouldn't learn till they had seen the dances, and as the dances are all for a number, it was impossible to show them till dancers had been found. It was difficult to reach the men. The Y.M.C.A. hut in each camp had its regular weekly programme: service, cinema, concert, lecture, and what not, and it was obviously impossible to ask for the use of a hut for an experiment which would mean no evening's entertainment for hundreds of men. One could use the concert hall in the morning, but the men were always at work, or, if off duty, would be at rest after a night's shift, and not at all inclined to take exercise.

The only thing to do was to make friends amongst the Association workers and the men, and to try to arouse interest and curiosity. Then perhaps one's friends would learn a few steps just for the sake of being pleasant. Two of the Y.M.C.A. ladies were already good dancers, having learned in England, but both were so busy that they could not give much time.

Someone suggested that a class would be welcomed at the Convalescent Depôt, and as the men were not on duty in the morning it would be possible to give classes without interfering with the evening programme. The hut leader sent a cordial invitation, and the experiment was tried.

It seemed best to begin with Northumbrian sword dances. The swords would make them less shy, as every man likes the feeling of a tool in his hand. One daren't teach Morris steps to men who were not well, and the hut was too crowded for a country dance. The men gathered round, and listened eagerly to the explanation and the invitation to come and be taught. Five stepped forward at once to take a sword each. Another volunteered to play the tune, and the lesson began. Everyone watched. Someone said, "That's the stuff to give 'em." No one laughed. Presently No.3 went a little pale and shiny, and said he must sit down, but someone else asked to take his place. No.3 said he was a heart case, but wanted to join in, and thought it would not matter. He held his head, and kept on looking pale. The teacher began to be frightened. Supposing someone else had a bad heart, and perhaps fell down dead! She stopped the class. No.5 said he had enjoyed it ever so much. He wanted to apologise for his bad dancing, but he had had a toe amputated, and was still in bandages, and his boots were new. The teacher went home. The hut leader was ever so nice, but thought the Convalescent Depôt was not the right place for folk dancing after all, as the men in the hut in the morning were not yet well enough for exercise, or they would, when one came to think of it, have been on duty on parade doing physical training under the gym.instructors.

But here and there a few friends had been found. Two men in one camp felt interested, they fetched four friends, and began to learn a long sword dance in the little class-room. After several lessons the four friends drifted away, but the two were left really keen, [sic] and desperately anxious to learn more, one saying that he had been so "fed up" with no definite interest for his spare time that he had often wondered what the end of it would be. Then there was a friend in another camp who had been in real life a teacher in an elementary school, and he had often thought how the men in camp would love the country dances, but had been too shy to begin to teach by himself.

There were two or three jolly country lads who had seen the old dances in their village, but were fearful of being laughed at if the others were watching. There were various

DAISY CAROLINE DAKING

Y.M.C.A. ladies working at the stores who would be glad of some game at the end of their long day over accounts.

The great need was some central room where everyone could meet and work together, and after much searching The Granary was found, the oddest, dirtiest place one had ever seen, with cobwebs and dust unimaginable, but an ideal place for country dancing. Everyone swept and dusted, and made things a little possible. The men volunteered for a fatigue, and swilled out the whole place, and it began to smell a little nicer.

Classes started and began to flourish. Men brought their friends and the Y.M.C.A. ladies came when they had a little spare time, which was not often. There was no furniture, and no piano, but the tin whistle and the comb and paper both make a cheerful noise, and later someone borrowed a fiddle, and then someone else came sometimes to play. Then at last a piano was secured, and after that the difficulties became much less, because one could at once demand a pianist, and a friend transferred to the new department to help with music and with everything else, and things began to feel quite happy and comfortable.

At the end of July there came the first demonstration. It was very bad indeed in that it was impossible to show either a sword dance or a Morris side, and the country dances were of the easiest. Everyone looked charming, the girls in blue and white striped frocks with blue tabards, and the men in cream shirts and the new baldrics. The audience went down before the novelty of the whole thing, and seemed to be lost in the spirit of it all. Sitting round the hut with the dancing space cleared in the centre, they seemed really able to imagine themselves on a village green in Blighty. They were told not to turn round, but to imagine that they were out of doors with the trees behind them. At the end some were persuaded to join the dancers, and be pulled through the Butterfly. The fun was then uproarious, and the performances ended in a storm of cheers, the men running the dancers' car all through the camp, and still cheering as it went down the road.

3. Group showing DCD with sword team at a
Convalescent Hospital in France.

4. The Cologne Central YMCA Folk-Dance Team
With DCD, her assistants and their hostess. 1919.

Soon the work was almost overwhelming, applications for classes and demonstrations coming from different huts round the base. It was arranged that one demonstration should be given every week, and the rest of the time devoted to class work, always insisting on the real point of making folk provide their own amusement rather than watch experts perform.

In some camps perhaps twenty or thirty would join the class, and really good country dancing resulted, with an attentive audience thoroughly enjoying the whole thing, and a demand for further lessons coming at the finish of the evening.

And the comments the men made were illuminating.

The big, rather solid man who said, after going through two or three longways dances, "I'm going to take this up, it will keep me off the booze." The little group in that other camp who said it had felt like paying a visit to Blighty. The rather old country man, who, after the lock had been tied, looked at it and said, "There's a lot behind this, more than you can see," so one told him a little about origins and folk-lore, and the rest crowded round to listen to the story.

This is an account of how our work began, and, considering the difficulties, it has certainly been encouraging.

There are now in France just twelve happy people working hard in our new department, and every one of them will assure you that, in spite of what other folk may say, this folk dancing is without a doubt the *very* best job in France.[17]

Her endless comings and goings cannot now be traced, though she seems to have been centred more or less on Le Havre and, after the Armistice, on Cologne. Certainly, from the spring of 1917 until well into 1919 she was incessantly travelling around behind the lines teaching folk-dancing to the troops, never staying anywhere or working with the same group for very long. She soon needed, and acquired, other helpers; some (like Helen Kennedy and Gladys Girdlestone) were sent out from England by the EFDS; others (like Lois Vidal) gave temporary help as and when they could. It was exhausting, frustrating, and immensely rewarding. DCD became surrogate aunt and mother to thousands, and loved them all.

After the Armistice in November 1918 she continued her work with the Army of occupation, in France and in the Rhineland, and seems not to have returned to England until well on in 1919. She was co-opted onto the committee of the EFDS in April 1918, but did not attend a meeting until 24 October 1919; thereafter her attendance was sporadic, as this was the period when she was travelling around the country for the YMCA, teaching, judging competitions and generally encouraging small groups of enthusiasts. A small YMCA booklet stuck into the *Log,* titled 'English Folk-Dancing. Men Women Boys Girls' must date from this period; she noted beneath it that

> this work lasted for two years & then had to be abandoned because lack of money meant the closing down of many Y.M.C.A. departments the Music Section included – but good work was done – the Lake District Branch was started off – one travelled Oxfordshire, Lincolnshire, Nottinghamshire, Cumberland & the Lakes & made many contacts & handed over little groups of enthusiasts to the E.F.D.S. But except for the Lake District the work mainly fizzled out. There was at that time no county organisation E.F.D.S. & one couldn't, therefore, hand over.

If, as seems likely, Oxenham's *The Abbey Girls Go Back to School* is set in 1920, then DCD attended the EFDS summer school at Cheltenham in August. It would certainly fit in with the picture given in that book of her wartime exploits being much talked of. The important account given of them there includes a description of her 'making over' an officers' mess, presumably described to Oxenham by a young officer, just as is done in the book.

It was probably at this summer school she first met Elsie Oxenham, who had become a member of the EFDS in April 1920, and who is our chief source for 'the Pixie's' movements for the next few years. Before Oxenham moved with her family to Worthing in 1922 she was much involved with folk-dancing in London, and her three Abbey books describing this milieu, though published 1923-25, relate to the years 1921-22.

By the winter of 1921-2 DCD had settled back in London, being particularly connected with the new big YMCA building in Plaistow (a war memorial), which was officially opened on 4 June 1921. Oxenham's account can therefore be corroborated by, and dated from, YMCA sources.

The New Abbey Girls (1923) has a quite detailed description of the Plaistow institute, making clear how recently 'the Pixie' has started her dance classes there - only a few weeks before a conversation taking place in March (1922). Oxenham had undoubtedly been to see the place for herself, and describes with enthusiasm the 'big white palace' with its 'wide double staircase, the entrance to the cinema close beside them, the glimpses of big lounge and billiard-rooms through open doors'. Then came the restaurant, a 'big hall, with its high windows, little tables, brown woodwork, and waiting-girls in brown with hanging veils to their caps.' Later 'the Pixie' shows the visitors the 'beautiful gymnasium' –

> "We dance here, on party nights. I play for them, up there!" pointing to the piano on its platform under the roof. "I go up the ladder. I'm always lifted down very tenderly off the last three steps by some of my men. It does amuse me so!" – to the billiard-rooms, with their big green tables and low, shaded lights – "Any one can have a game here by paying a little. It's not only for club-members. Much better than going to the public-house for your game, you know!" – to the big lounge and reading-room, the boys' club-room and the girls' club-room, with their huge red-brick open hearths, restful brown wooden furniture, big red leather easy-chairs and settees, tables with papers and magazines, and cosy corners arranged for discussions; - to the cinema-theatre; and last of all to the big swimming-pool, used during the day by the schools of the neighbourhood, and at night open to members of the clubs.[18]

In the next book we learn how the swimming-pool is covered over in winter, renamed the Hydro Hall, and used for parties, something which YMCA sources date to the winter of 1922-3.

Mention is made of 'the Pixie's' portable gramophone, and also of her playing a tin whistle for the dancing. One of the stories later incorporated into *Jen of the Abbey School* tells us that she had acquired a Basque pipe during her time in France, although she couldn't play it properly. In *The New Abbey Girls* she plays the whistle for a 'men's' morris class; the visitors are astonished that she calls her class 'men' and she has to explain that the small size of the lads of eighteen is due to poor housing conditions and diet.

DAISY CAROLINE DAKING

5. Artist's impression of the new Plaistow YMCA building, 1921.

But she is adamant that

"And yet they can take as much and as deep delight in a purely artistic thing like folk-dancing as any of your West Enders. You saw how they loved it; and the girls are the same in their country-dancing. You should see the joy, and life, and energy in our Saturday night parties! I never saw heartier dancing. They'd tire you out in one evening. And yet they're City people; shows 'country' dancing isn't really the best name. It's because it's folk, of course; folk-dancing. It appeals to everybody; that's folk. It's sincere and natural, and they all respond to it, just as the Tommies did in France. My lot here simply love it. They have modern dancing too, but they like our parties best; they've told me so. And they love it in the best way; their dancing is as artistic, and as musical, and as full of rhythm and beautiful movement, and of delight in it all, as any you'd find anywhere, even at your Vacation

THE FINE COMPANION

Schools or big town classes. But you've seen the streets they come from; only the big streets, of course! You don't know anything about their homes, really; but you've seen enough for a beginning; and you've seen the results in them. Those are our 'men'; those little slips of lads, with no height or growth to speak of; that's Plaistow! I love them, and I love being here. And they like me, you know! ... Now, good-bye, everybody!" and she ran down the steps to her own room, a tiny, eager figure in fawn knitted coat over smooth black tunic, black band round smooth fair hair.[19]

Later in the same book we are given a description of one of the parties at Plaistow by 'the Writing Person', Oxenham's way of putting herself into her own book:

"... They all dance fearfully hard, and the Pixie, in a white frock, stands up on the high platform under the roof and acts as M.C., and shouts orders in a voice that every one can hear; and if there's too much noise she uses a whistle. When she wants to come down, she clings to the rope and runs down the ladder, and some big man, or two or three men, lift her off and deposit her tenderly on the floor. Then she runs round and arranges the sets, and hustles everybody into the places *she* thinks would be best for them, and breaks up the little cliques, if they're beginning to form, and nobody minds; they'll all do anything for her. She simply won't stand cliques. If you go to her parties, you've got to be ready to dance with anybody and go just where she thinks you'll be most help to those who don't know the dances well. You really haven't any choice in the matter. But then you don't want it. You feel, as they do, that you'll do any mortal thing she wants, if only it will help her. And you've only got to look at any of those men and girls to see how much they think of her."[20]

Lastly *The New Abbey Girls* gives us a discus-

sion of the need to share whatever one has with whoever
has not, with 'the Pixie' as a prime example:

> "... I knew I felt a slacker if I didn't go shares, and
> I've been feeling it more and more strongly since that visit
> to Plaistow. I'm sure the Pixie would echo every word
> you've said; she lives it all, every day! The rest teach danc-
> ing because they want everybody to have it because they
> love it so much for itself; but *she* teaches it because she
> loves the men and girls in her classes so much that she must
> give them the best she knows. She teaches for love of the
> girls and men – particularly the men! The rest teach for love
> of their subject."[21]

DCD's evenings seem to have been fully occupied by her Plaistow YMCA classes, and she was also
teaching school-teachers, who then passed their knowledge on to their pupils. Oxenham records that she was
sharing a flat somewhere off Theobalds Road with a
shorthand typist and a policewoman, but sleeping when
necessary at Plaistow in the university settlement there;

In *The Abbey Girls Again* (1924), which is set
only a few weeks after its predecessor, Oxenham describes how 'the Pixie' is now working in a 'little West
End shop' (so not Liberty's, as has been sometimes
supposed). 'I can't afford to do nothing all day' she
says, making it clear that her classes only took place at
night. Again, Oxenham had clearly visited her at work,
for there is a vivid description of the shop, workroom
and the girl weavers who produce the wonderful fabrics
sold there:

> On the little counter, on the shelves behind, and on
> the ledges against the opposite wall, were piles of beautiful
> handwoven materials, in vivid, or delicate, or soft shades of

colour. In one corner, in an open cupboard, were heaped spools of thread and wool and silk ready for use on the looms. The Pixie pulled out piece after piece of the finished goods and spread them on the counter ...[22]

'The Pixie' herself does not do the weaving; her job is upstairs, designing and making dresses. Evidently her needlework skills were considerable; as early as the *Log of the 'Fine Companion'* she records herself making nightgowns for her infant nephew. Sewing would of course have been a normal part of any girl's upbringing, and Oxenham's books show her as responding aesthetically to the colours around her, something later touched on in her works on psychology.

In the same book there is what is evidently an eye-witness account of a big children's party at Plaistow, the children being the pupils of the teachers DCD had taught for two terms. *The Red Triangle* included a brief description in its number for April 1923:

PLAISTOW

Miss Daking organized a wonderfully successful folk-dance party for children in March. Over 160 children from the local schools were present in the Hydro Hall, and charmed a large audience with old English dances. Miss Daking has been training over thirty school teachers, in folk dancing, weekly for two terms, in the Red Triangle Club, and this party was the outcome of their work in the schools.

Oxenham, who must have been present, gives us a much more detailed description:

The big swimming-bath was transformed into a dancing hall. Parents and friends hung over the balcony

30

DAISY CAROLINE DAKING

6. The swimming bath at the Plaistow YMCA,
National Swimming & Water Polo Championships, Sept. 1923

railing. Small girls in frocks of every rainbow colour filled the hall. Where the frocks, and big hair-ribbons, and white stockings, and coloured shoes, had come from it was difficult to imagine, for the children were from poor schools in East Ham and Canning Town and Barking. Already they were fairly jumping with excitement, racing about wildly to find friends or call greetings to mothers up aloft; new groups kept arriving to swell the crowd. The Pixie, a vivid green spot, seemed in every corner at once, like a very active fairy in a world of brilliant butterflies.

The pianist played the air of "Galopede", and with a wild rush from every corner of the hall, every child was on the spot assigned to her, thrilled to the limit, desperately determined that not one moment should be lost.

"Eight times through!" announced the Pixie, appearing suddenly on the platform, and piano and violin struck up the tune.[23]

31

And so on. Galopede is followed by Rufty Tufty, then by Gathering Peascods and The Butterfly, Winifred's Knot and The Black Nag, We Won't go Home till Morning and finally Sellenger's Round. At one point comes an incident which surely confirms that Oxenham was present:

> It was after the next dance that some small person, sitting on the shining floor to rest, discovered that by lifting up her feet and giving herself a push with her hands, she could spin round and round like a top. The fashion spread like measles, and in every corner little rings of small girls sat twirling happily, ignoring agitated parents, who could not forget the certain results to white underclothes.
> "Oh, look! *Look* at them!" the Pixie was almost helpless with laughter. "And Mother's up in the gallery telling them not to! They won't listen, of course! Look, they're all doing it! It's as good as the dancing! Oh, aren't they simply priceless?"[24]

The last Oxenham book of this group, *The Abbey Girls in Town* (1925), describing the events of the following winter, has 'the Pixie' taking part in the EFDS Christmas vacation school at the Chelsea Polytechnic, but we do not hear anything of her work.

She served on the Committee of the EFDS from 1918 till 1926, when she resigned immediately after the death of Cecil Sharp. She had not taken very much part in the work of the Committee, though she was clearly acting as liaison with the YMCA, and she may not have been in sympathy with its other members; it was a period of difficulty for the Society and DCD appears to have distanced herself from it after Sharp's death.[25]

DAISY CAROLINE DAKING

Her address in the EFDS members' lists from the late 1920s into the 1930s is at various places in London. Her Maxwell uncle and aunt had by now retired from Barnet to Abinger Hammer in Surrey, and she had been able to purchase the plot next to their new bungalow and move the van onto it. *Queen of the Abbey Girls* (1926) describes a visit made by fictional Jen which is so detailed that we can safely assume that it was in reality made by Oxenham herself.

By this date (no later than 1925, and probably a year or two earlier) the van had been taken off its wheels and stood at the top of a slope on a concrete platform. The setting is idyllic: the visitor alights from the bus 'at a village with a pond, and ducks, and a big clock and a little figure of a man, who came out every hour to strike the bell with a hammer' (recognisably Abinger Hammer), and then, after a drive 'past the duck-pond and across the common and down a winding lane with high banks' comes a disappointment:

> In spite of warnings, she had expected to see a gaily-painted caravan, high on its wheels. The long narrow field stretching up the hill, with knee-high grass and buttercups and sorrel, had a kind of shed-arrangement at its higher end, on a little bank; it looked like a bit of fencing on an allotment. … A tiny rustic gate bore a wooden name-board, "Robin's Rest." The path within it led down a bank to a single plank which bridged a swift little stream; an oak tree by the brook stretched its arms over the lower field and gave the only shade.[26]

Once within the wooden fence the Van is revealed:

THE FINE COMPANION

7. Probable site of the van, Abinger, Surrey, 2010.
The van will have stood at the top of the slope to the left.
The neighbouring bungalow is partly visible on the right.

> The caravan had no wheels, so seemed strangely low down, for a caravan. It was sitting on a broad concrete platform, its door open to the hillside, its back to the road down in the valley. The fence ... stood screening it from the road, so that it was invisible to any one approaching until the corner of the screen was passed. This extra wall ... stood several feet from the Van, the space between roofed in, so that there was room for a wooden cupboard, a meat-safe, tables and shelves; jars and pails stood below, for storage or for washing-up purposes.'[27]

No mention is made of sanitary arrangements, either here or earlier; as far as the Surrey plot goes we can only hope that the Maxwells next-door provided at least a bathroom, replacing the tent and – was it a tin tub? – mentioned in the *Log*. In Surrey there is a tap half-way down the field; on the road water must have had to be fetched from wherever was nearest.

DAISY CAROLINE DAKING

Inside the van *Queen of the Abbey Girls* tells us about a hanging table, corner cupboard, broad seat along one side containing storage space, and two-tier bunk beds, of which the top one can be lifted off and moved outside. Oil-stove and lamp provide cooking, heat and light. In pre-electricity, pre-modern sanitation days the van was no worse than many cottages (though they at least might have had an earth-closet), and for summer camping sounds comfortable and, in Oxenham's description and fine weather, idyllic. The *Log* is more realistic when it comes to wet days, mentioning rubber boots, waterproofs, and a leaking roof, not things on which Oxenham was ever wont to lay stress.

A throw-away line in *Queen of the Abbey Girls* shows Daking expecting a visit from 'some of the Kibboo Kift'. This movement (usually called the Kibbo Kift) had begun in the East End (where DCD probably encountered it) in 1920 with the aim of regenerating society and with great emphasis on outdoor education and the open air; later on it developed into the Green Shirt Movement for Social Credit with distinctly Fascist overtones. Many people left it because of these political developments, and DCD may have been one – we really know nothing about her involvement with it except that members came down to camp on at least this one occasion. We have no knowledge at all of her political affiliations, but her sympathies seem always to have been with the working rather than the privileged classes.

Queen of the Abbey Girls is the last detailed source for DCD's movements, either as herself or as 'the Pixie'. A few bare facts are recorded in the annals of the EFDS. Whether the van was retained we simply do not know, but DCD's addresses from then on are at various places in London, with one diversion in 1935 to Whitstable. This is now known to be an aunt's house; one aunt died there in 1934 and another seems to have lived there until her own death in 1940. (These were Ashby relations, her mother's sisters.) It was remembered by her family that DCD worked as a cook in various places, which gives an unhappy sensation that she was having to do whatever she could to earn a living. Folk-dancing had ceased to pay, and it sounds as though the hand-made woven dresses had also come to an end. Emily Maxwell, 'Auntie', died in 1934, and 'Uncle' remarried; this may have made relations with him more distant.

In 1932 she published a short work, *Feed My Sheep*, and in 1933 the longer *Jungian Psychology and Modern Spiritual Thought*, both dealing with psychology and issued by the rather obscure Anglo-Eastern Publishing Company of London. They show her interested in religion as well as psychology, indeed, attempting to reconcile the two, but without making a definite commitment to any particular Christian church. She had read, and approved, the work of Denys Prideaux, the Anglo-Catholic Abbot of Nashdom (then still at Pershore), and seems to have encountered Dr J.D. Hessey, a doctor who in the years around 1930 is recorded as speaking in Christ Church, Victoria Street, London, on such subjects as 'Shall we recognize each other in the Hereafter?', 'The Psychology of Life', and 'Spiritual Healing'; these tie in quite closely with *Jungian Psychology*. DCD bequeathed Hessey her diaries, suggesting a close connection; unfortunately there is no record of whether this bequest was ever carried out, or, if so, what happened to the diaries.

At this time DCD was in some way involved with a young man, possibly the Thomas Smith to whom she dedicated *Jungian Psychology,* 'because he took care of my punctualities',[28] and to whom she left £100 in her will; his address in 1935 was, like hers, 1 Somerset Terrace, Dukes Road, London; by 1940, when she added a codicil, he had married and was living in Herne Bay. The relationship seems to have been one of patronage on DCD's part, even quasi-adoption, but family tradition says that he disappointed her in some way. Her relationship with him also damaged her relationship with her nephew.

On the outbreak of the Second World War in 1939 DCD clearly hoped to repeat her work in the First, but was gently discouraged by Douglas Kennedy.[29] She was presumably still living in London at this point, and apparently still in touch with the EFDS, but on 27 September 1940 Cecil Sharp House suffered bomb damage, bringing activities to at least a temporary halt.

By May 1942 DCD was working in Oxford as superintendent of a girls' hostel. We know now that she had had a breakdown in 1915 after a period of hard work and following the shattering blow of the outbreak of the First War. Now she seems to have had another, brought on by a combination of depression at the progress and effects of the war, sadness at the failure of her relationship with 'Thomas Smith', and hurt at the rejection of her third book. She died by her own hand on 10 May 1942.

THE FINE COMPANION

When this became known it was a shock to those who knew her only as 'the Pixie' in Oxenham's books, where she is shown as a strong character coping gallantly with the difficulties of life. But Oxenham's friendship with her seems to have ended some fourteen years before her death, and in the intervening years DCD's world and perhaps her opinions had changed. It may help to find what she wrote in *Jungian Psychology* about 'the Otherness', her name for what she felt existed beyond human experience:

> ... in this Otherness, is the cool clarity of the star-shine far above the trees tops on a frosty night. My soul reaches to this, feels a tranquillity in the very act of reaching, feels, therefore, at home.
> ... It [the afterlife] is not restless, not violent, not lost nor frightening. There is nothing that lawless and incertain thoughts could by any possibility imagine. It is a cool clarity of peace and it is a darkly shining radiance and not a nothingness. Rather, a Something that is the great difference from all that we at present know. It is a Somethingness that once you have experienced you are always and consciously ready for. Happily ready, I mean: so happily ready that you do not take the trouble to long for or look forward to.
> For the knowledge of it makes Actuality so amusing and such fun. Our play and our work, the past and the present and the future, birth and death, all so orderly and so small: you love them so tenderly for their smallness and their orderliness.
> But this Otherness, it is beyond your mere soul, outside it. And your soul reaches out, turns towards this Otherness.[30]

If this is what she believed she was going to, it helps us to understand why, in the depths of despair, she took the means to depart.

DAISY CAROLINE DAKING

It is a dark end to a brave story, but we can take comfort that her joy in folk-dancing, gallant acceptance until the very end of all that life threw at her, and wise advice to others, have earned her a certain immortality. Who knows what her unrecorded influence over the soldiers in the First War and the young people she taught in Plaistow may have been? We may safely say of her: she made a difference, and a difference very much for the good. She had indeed been a 'fine companion'.

1. Since 1932 the English Folk Dance and Song Society.
2. Daking, *Jungian Psychology & Modern Spiritual Thought,* pp.99-100
3. *op.cit.,* pp.100-101.
4. e.g. Oxenham, *The Abbey Girls go back to School*, p.202.
5 *The Oxford Journal*, 20 March 1912.
6. Marjorie Sidgwick, *EFDS News* No. 22, 1930
7. Vidal, *Magpie,* p.60
8. Oxenham, t*he Abbey Girls Go Back to School*, 1922,p.193
9. She also appears in *Jen of the Abbey School* (1927), which derives from earlier short stories (see Bibliography).
10. As DCD succeeded Peggy Walsh as teacher in Oxford (see Appendix C) the demonstrators, including Tiddy, may well have learned to dance before she arrived.
11. Oxenham, *The Abbey Girls go Back to School*, p.303.
12. Report of the Oxford branch of the EFDS, quoted in Roy Judge, *The Ancient Men: the OUMM and its background.*
13. Vidal, *Magpie*, p.65.
14. *EFDS Journal*, 1915.
15. Vidal, *Magpie*, p.84.
16. Vidal, *Magpie*, pp.83-85.
17. *The Red Triangle*, July 1918, pp.446-448.
18. Oxenham, *The New Abbey Girls*, pp.192-3
19. *op.cit.*, pp.199-202.
20. *op.cit.* pp.244-5
21. *op.cit.* pp.273-4

THE FINE COMPANION

22. Oxenham, *The Abbey Girls Again*, p.286.
23. *op.cit.*, pp.134-6.
24. *op.cit.* p.144
25. Confirmed by Douglas Kennedy's obituary of DCD
    in *English Dance and Song*, June 1942, where he says
    that 'her appearances at meetings and parties were rare
    events in recent years'.
26. Oxenham, *Queen of the Abbey Girls*, pp.222-228.
27. *op.cit.* p.229
28. Her punctuation? The *Log* shows that it was not entirely
    orthodox, and her spelling was unreliable.
29. His reply is pasted into the *Log*.
30. Daking, *Jungian Psychology*, pp.132-3.

THE OTHER 'FINE COMPANIONS'

'P'

To identify 'P', the second 'Fine Companion', as Gladys Marguerite Girdlestone may at first sight seem somewhat perverse. But that 'P' was named Girdlestone is clear from the telegram sent to the Companions by Alec on 4 August 1914, which is addressed to 'Daking-Girdlestone', and one of the photographs of the caravan party stuck into the *Log* includes 'G. Girdlestone' in its caption. On 26 July DCD recorded cycling to Iffley 'to see P', which tallies with what we know about Gladys Girdlestone's home.

'P' therefore evidently stands for a nickname or pet name, and the most obvious solution is that Gladys Marguerite Girdlestone was habitually known by her second name which, as a version of Margaret, might have been shortened to Peggy or Peg. It is worth remembering that DCD herself was officially Caroline Daisy but always been called Daisy.

Gladys Marguerite Girdlestone was born at Harley Lodge, Clifton Park, Bristol, on 1 November 1884, some two months after DCD. Her father was Francis Brook Girdlestone, at the time of her birth general manager of the Bristol Docks, following service in the East India Company's India Navy and as a surveyor in the

THE FINE COMPANION

8. The 'Fine Companion' on the road.
DCD driving, 'P' (?) with bicycle.

Indian Topographical Survey Department. Attacks of
jungle fever brought that phase of his life to an end, and
in 1875 he was appointed secretary of the Bristol Docks,
becoming general manager in 1884. On his retirement in
1911 he settled with his family in the Mill House at
Iffley, near Oxford, later moving into the city to a house
in St Margaret's Road in North Oxford, and at the very
end of his life to Ridgway, Headington Hill. Gathorne
Girdlestone, the pioneering orthopaedic surgeon, was
a cousin and is now commemorated by a road near his
foundation, the Nuffield Hospital in Headington.

The Girdlestones were clearly in comfortable
circumstances, and there would have been no need for

'P' to earn her own living. We know nothing about her education except that she played the piano well (at least in DCD's estimation). In the summer of 1914, aged twenty-nine, she was evidently residing with her parents and following her interest in folk-dancing, which is presumably what brought her and DCD together. She had gained her Elementary Certificate from the EFDS before the end of 1913, and got her Advanced Certificate in 1914. During the 1914-18 war she worked for the Red Cross at Boulogne and subsequently joined DCD in teaching folk-dancing to the troops in France, her particular work being at the big convalescent depôt at Etaples. After the war she was for a time involved in organising big folk-dance parties in Hyde Park.

Immediately after the Armistice, however, on 24 January 1919, she married David Abernethy Donaldson, a 'commercial artist' some six years her junior, who was then a sergeant and stationed at Boulogne but whose home address was in Edinburgh, where the couple were married. Their son Francis (presumably called after her father) was born later that year, and they seem to have lived for some time at Sible Hedingham in Essex. In the mid 1920s they appear to have been based with her parents in Oxford (her father died in 1926) but after that their movements are uncertain.

Gladys Donaldson died on 20 December 1966, in Sussex, her address at the time of making her will in 1961 being Rosers Cross, Waldron. Nothing more is known of her life, nor whether she retained an interest in folk-dancing and her friendship with DCD. David Donaldson became a journalist, dying in Edinburgh in 1975. Their son Francis served during WW2 with the

THE FINE COMPANION

Special Operations Executive, but his later career has not been traced.

Although 'P' is recorded as having kept a diary of the *Fine Companion* trip, it has not been possible to find out whether it survives.

9. The 'fine companions' relaxing in camp.
DCD, Alec, 'P'

'ALEC'

ALEXANDER Noel Hepburne-Scott,[1] to give him his full name, was the second son of an aristocratic Scottish family of illustrious lineage and connections. At the time of his birth, on 14 October 1892, his father was Master of Polwarth, in other words was the heir to the barony of Polwarth. (As his paternal grandfather did not die until 1920 Alec never bore the style of 'the Honourable' which would have been his had he survived until his father inherited the title.)

The young Hepburne-Scotts lived principally at Humbie, East Lothian, on the edge of the Lammermuirs, and Alec was both born and christened there. His second name, Noel, was given him both after his mother's brother and because he was baptised on Christmas Day.

There were seven Hepburne-Scott children. Alec had an elder brother, Walter (Wattie), and an elder sister, Helen, while below him came Margaret (a year and a half younger), Patrick (six years younger), Christian and Grisell (nearly nine and ten years younger respectively); he thus fell very much into the elder half of the family, though the siblings were united and mutually affectionate.

His education followed an orthodox pattern, slightly modified because as a child he was considered small and delicate. Nursery education at home, and at a kindergarten in Edinburgh when the family were there for a winter, was followed by five years in the junior department of Edinburgh Academy, where he was a weekly boarder. Then came his public school, Repton, and eventually Balliol College, Oxford, to which he went in the Michaelmas term of 1911 to read History, a contemporary of the future Prime Minister Harold Macmillan (though there is no record of them ever having met). The family memoir published after his death shows him as musical and thoughtful, not apparently a games player, but lively and much loved. He was something of a linguist, and made the most of continental travels with his family, learning both German and French; he seems to have been considering a career in the consular service, for which of course languages would have been essential. He seems to have met folk-dancing at Oxford (though he would probably have learned Scottish dancing from infancy) and to have taken to it enthusiastically: in the summer of 1914 he was in the top class at the EFDS summer school, which suggests considerable competence.

Illustrious as was his father's family (Sir Walter Scott himself was of a younger branch of the Polwarth branch of the Scotts of Buccleuch), his mother's and maternal grandmother's were equally so. His mother, Edith Frances Buxton, was the eldest daughter of Sir Thomas Fowell Buxton, 3rd baronet, and philanthropist, descended from Thomas Fowell Buxton the anti-slavery campaigner; her mother, Alec's grandmother, Victoria Noel, was the youngest daughter of the 1st Earl of Gainsborough and herself a noted philanthropist. She was the mother of the politician Noel Buxton (later Lord Noel-Buxton), from whom Alec took his second name, and the aunt of the Rev. Conrad Noel, the controversial socialist vicar of Thaxted whose parish became a heady mix of socialism, folk-dancing and high church ritual. Alec visited there in the summer of 1913 and was impressed:

> ... I cycled from Thaxted, about 30 miles. It was really rather fun there. They had a huge demonstration, procession, high Mass, &c. Of course it all appeared very spikey to us of Protestant prejudice, but it was awfully interesting, and I thought very highly of it all. There was a huge procession, lots of banners carried by men in robes surrounded by girls with flowers, &c. There were swarms of clergy in robes and copes, &c, lots of boys waving censers of smoking incense. They were in terrible fear of being wrecked and routed by the Kensitites. Crowds assembled, but did nothing more than laugh, &c. They wanted me to walk in the procession, which I did for a short way, but a lady asked me half-way through if I was a Church Socialist, to which I answered, "Neither." That rather put me off, so I left the procession and watched them go into the church. The service was wonderful. They don't stick at anything. The ordinary Matins is done away with, and its place taken by High Mass. A few people walked out, but nothing more exciting. On the Saturday evening there was Morris-dancing in the vicarage garden. We had some ordinary dancing too. The girls were the most interesting partners I have had for a long time. They talked hard about all sorts of things. I am sure this democratic teaching of Conrad's, combined with Morris-dancing, &c., has done a tremendous lot for them. They say that this change has only come in the last two years. I know of no other place in the world where the village people are so interesting and sensible. Obviously they are having rather a struggle, and one cannot help disliking their attitude towards dissenters, coupled with their obvious self-pride, but it is so pleasant to find people who are not afraid to do something. The average parson and bishop are always afraid to take any side.

THE FINE COMPANION

All his family connections, therefore, were cultured, liberal and philanthropic, and Alec's own gentleness and slightly unconventional opinions reflected theirs.

Nevertheless, the outbreak of war on 4 August 1914 swept him away into the ranks of the army. If youthful enthusiasm led him to enlist so quickly, his family's heritage of public service was not going to discourage him, and much as they must have feared for him they were also proud of him. Six weeks after joining up he was on his way to France, and his parents and younger brother and sister came to see him on his way.

In the eight months of life remaining to him loving letters and parcels followed him, and in 1916 his eldest nephew, whom he did not live to see, was given the second name Alexander. In 1919 his parents had his letters privately printed for the family 'so that it may be easy to read them often, and so his memory may be kept ever fresh by us all'. It was this action which has indeed kept his memory fresh and brings before us the lively young man of whom his family and friends wrote with such heart-breaking affection.

From the letters we are able to reconstruct his version of the time he spent with the 'Fine Companion'. It came at the moment that he was at a loose end, having just sat his final examinations ('Schools' in Oxford slang) in History and presumably not thinking it worth while to join his family in Scotland because he wanted to go to the Folk Dance summer school in August.

He spent some time at Hove with 'Teddy' Jones (the 'Rufty' of the Log), a Balliol friend, whose father was suffragan Bishop of Lewes, and went from there to other friends in Warwick, with the intention of visiting others and perhaps walking in the Cotwolds. Just before his Oxford viva he stayed in London with his friend William Watson, mentioned in the *Log* as the motor-cyclist who failed to catch the 'Fine Companion' at Banbury on 29 July. When Watson came to write his wartime memoirs, he opened them with precision:

'At 6.45 p.m. on Saturday, July 25, 1914, Alec and I determined to take part in the Austro-Servian War. I remember the exact minute, because we were standing on the "down" platform of Earl's Court Station, waiting for the 6.55 through train to South Harrow, and Alec had just re-marked that we had ten minutes to wait. We had travelled up to London, intending to work in the British Museum for our "vivas" at Oxford, but in the morning it had been so hot that we had strolled round Bloomsbury, smoking our pipes. By lunch-time we had gained such an appetite that we did not feel like work in the afternoon. We went to see Elsie Janis.

The evening papers were full of grave prognostica-tions. War between Servia and Austria seemed inevitable. Earl's Court Station inspired us with the spirit of adventure. We determined to take part, and debated whether we should go out as war correspondents or as orderlies in a Servian hospital. At home we could talk of nothing else during dinner. Ikla, that wisest of Egyptians, mildly encour-aged us, while the family smiled.

On Sunday we learned that war had been declared. Ways and means were discussed, but our great tennis tour-nament on Monday and a dance in the evening, left us with a mere background of warlike endeavour. It was vaguely determined that when my "viva" was over we should go and see people of authority in London.'[2]

Alec must have gone from London to Oxford and then to Burford, for he took part in the folk-dance demonstration there on 27 July, as he wrote to his mother:

> We had a great day yesterday. Cecil Sharp came down, and there was a big Morris show. The London performers came down, and as they were a man short, they asked me to dance with them in some things. After the performance there was general country dancing in the open air. It was great fun, and appears to have done a lot of good. They have just started a branch here, and are doing well. Sharp and all his people are still here…

His viva was on 28 July, after which he planned to go to Stratford, as he had earlier written to his sister:

> I have practically fixed to go to Stratford-on-Avon till 8th August. It is what I have meant to do these last two years, but have been unable. I am very keen to go, as Folk-dancing is my real hobby, and I am very interested in the whole thing. A week's hard work at it will make all the difference. My Viva is on the 28th, so the three intervening days I shall spend on the trek from Oxford to Stratford, all through very good country.

Following Stratford he had an invitation to visit friends in Oban, and had plans to try for the Consular service in August 1915, requiring a time in France followed by some serious cramming. Joining the Austro-Servian War seems to have receded into the background, for from Stratford, on 2 August (date inferred from the *Log of the Fine Companion*), he wrote home:

> I will send you the "log" I have been keeping during the caravan trip – that will save writing about it all again. It has been absolutely perfect. I have never had three such

priceless days. We were up on the top of Edgehill, and came in yesterday morning – twelve miles' walk with the van, after getting up at 6 and packing all the tents, &c. I wish I was camping here. You, I suppose, at home think me quite mad coming to dance here. I admit it must be difficult to understand it. Of course, there is more than the mere dancing – there is a lot in the Folk movement. It is going to be awfully good fun. I am in the top class, which is small, most of them being good teachers keen to work at it. We begin at 9 and work all morning, and then an hour after tea. It has poured all morning. I went to church – music and service good. I am down at Miss D. and Miss G.'s camp now. I helped them to put up their tents, and worked hard here last night, in return for which they wash and mend my socks, &c., which are in a lamentable condition. This war is awful – things are bad, and yet I don't see how we can go to war. We have no interests at all. If only Germany were not such a military oligarchy. I have complete trust in the Government. We may be thankful the Tories are not in – what a mess there would be. We have a perfect Prime Minister, Foreign Minister, War Minister, and Navy Minister. That makes all the difference. Do write suggestions about my plans. I find it very difficult. Expect me home Monday, 10th. I cannot leave here till Saturday afternoon. …

But two days later, as soon as Britain declared war, he wired home *What do you advise doing?* and then *Joining London Scottish.*

Clearly, like so many other young men, he was swept away by the general excitement. His companion at this point was 'Teddy' Jones ('Rufty' in the *Log of the 'Fine Companion'*) who also joined up in the ranks of the London Scottish but who within a few days fell sick and was discharged. It was while visiting Teddy's fiancée, Kathleen Scott (no relation) and her family in Blackheath that Alec acquired some kit to supplement official inadequacies – he did have a kilt, and a khaki tunic, but was given various items including *whole stockings of the right colour* by Kathleen's father, who had been in the London Scottish himself.

Within a few days, though he wrote quite cheerfully, he was evidently wondering whether he ought to go in for a commission; by the end of the month he thought he should go to the Scottish Horse, where he would be of most use; otherwise he would stick with the London Scottish *and go* [to France] *when they go*. (His father had evidently been advocating the 8th Royal Scots, but Alec thought they probably wouldn't now have a vacancy.)

Barely had the plans for the Scottish Horse been settled, however, when in fact he was off with 800 of the London Scottish, writing home from France on 18 September. His French came in useful, and he was able to feel superior to various monoglot officers:

> but one must try and behave like a private! Personally, I find it quite impossible. I suppose it is that shadow of Balliol, or "the sublime sense of effortless superiority" (in the words of the Prime Minister), that makes it unattainable.

By 7 October he had been to Nantes and back, still in good spirits, and shortly after that ended up as telephonist to the Railway Transport Officer in Abbeville, his fluent French evidently coming in useful. By 24 October he had moved on, reporting that the natives were bemused by the sight of the kilted Scots, and lamenting the loss of kit and missing letters.

By early November he was in Ypres, then in Bailleul, and finally arrived at the front, where they stayed in the trenches for five days. Fallen back behind the lines he reported receiving numerous parcels from friends and family, and meeting various acquaintances.

He seems to have been back in the trenches early in January, for he reported leaving them on the 11th, and on the 13th having slept with his boots off for the first time for a month. By now he was hearing of the death of friends, and the full misery of war was biting home.

10. 2nd Lt.. A.N. Hepburne-Scott

On 20 January he was in hospital with jaundice, and then was sent home. He was finally gazetted 2nd Lieutenant in the Scots Guards, and spent time in

THE FINE COMPANION

Cornwall and London. Early in April he was off to France again, and by the beginning of May was back in the trenches, though apparently in a sector with nothing much happening, as he complained of boredom. By mid-May things were moving again, and on 16 May he was killed in an attack at Ypres.

It was the story of thousands of young men, swept up into a horror they had not anticipated, each loss as poignant to their friends and families as Alec's was. He does seem to have been especially beloved, and because he was killed so relatively early the shock of his loss was all the greater.

William Watson, who had intended joining the London Scottish with Alec and Teddy Jones, got diverted and signed on as a motor-cyclist. He survived, despite passing into the Tank Corps and ending up as a major with the DSO and DSM. He dedicated his first book to Alec's memory, and wrote to Mrs Scott

> Alec did me the great honour of calling me one of his friends. This was a fine privilege, because Alec was made for friendship. he was always loyal and always kind; I do not think I ever heard him say an unkind word about anybody. He seemed instinctively to look for the good in people, and because he looked for it he found it. But though he was loyal and kind and sweet-charactered, he was the best company in the world; full of life and laughter, and a queer little wit. A dinner or gathering of any kind was never quite the same if Alec were not there. His gaiety, like his kindness, was epidemic.
>
> .... This war is making life bitter. It has taken several of my friends. Alec was the hardest blow, because when I was with him I felt that, under the grace of God, I must some day become a good man.

'ALEC'

In the 'Introductory letter to 2nd Lt. R.B.Whyte, 1st Black Watch, B.E.F. († Sept.1915)' of his book, *Adventures of a Despatch Rider,* p.x: he wrote:

> We have known together two of the people I have mentioned in this book – Alec and Gibson.
>
> They have both advanced so far that we have lost touch with them. I had thought that it would be a great joy to publish a first book, but this book is ugly with sorrow. I shall never be able to write "Alec and I" again – and he was the sweetest and kindest of my friends, a friend of all the world. Never did he meet a man or woman that did not love him. The Germans have killed Alec ….'

Alec has no grave. His name is on the Le Touret Memorial in the military cemetery of that name at Richebourg-l'Avoue, commemorating those whose bodies were never found. This of course was a source of extra agony to his family: that of not knowing exactly what had happened to him, though his father did eventually manage to find a private who was there when Alec was wounded and then hit by a shell.

The letters his parents received after his death from his many friends show that he was remembered with great love, as someone really special. It seems appropriate to end with a quotation from a letter written by his cousin, Noel Ponsonby, which describes Alec the folk-dancer:

> … Then there came the craze for Morris-dancing. My friend, R.J.E.Tiddy, a don of Trinity and a delightful man (who has also been killed), got me to join them. We finally gave a public performance before hundreds of people in Oxford. We were all dressed in the correct costumes. Alec looked so beautiful in white, with gold bells and silk

coloured ribbons flying from his arms and legs. He danced
uncommonly well, and loved it.

Perhaps Alec should be counted among the legen-
dary lost folk-dancers, like Tiddy and Butterworth;
perhaps, had he survived, he would have grown away
from the movement. But thanks to the *Log of the 'Fine
Companion'* he can now be remembered as one of the
most appealing of the generation whose golden youth
came to an abrupt end on 4 August 1914.

1. Most of the information about Alec's life comes from
   *Alexander Noel Hepburne-Scott, 1892-1915. Letters to his
   mother and a few others.* This was privately printed for
   his family 'so that his memory may be kept ever fresh
   by us all', and I am grateful to the Polwarth and Capron
   families for permission to use this work.
2. W.H.L.Watson, *Adventures of a Despatch Rider*, pp.1-2.

PEOPLE

mentioned in the *Log of the 'Fine Companion'*

Marked * in text of the *Log.*

Balls, James William

'Mr Ball', as DCD calls him, was the farmer at Yatscombe Farm on Boar's Hill, probably the one now called Chilswell Farm.

Blunt, Miss Janet Heatley

See Michael Pickering, *Village Song & Culture*, a study based on the Blunt Collection of song from Adderbury, North Oxfordshire, 1982, also "Janet Blunt – Folk Song Collector & Lady of the Manor" *Folk Music Journal*, vol. 3, no.2, 1976, pp.114-149. Full text in unpublished PhD thesis, *The Passing of a Community and its Songs*, Institute. of Dialect & Folk Life Studies, University of Leeds 1978.

Janet Heatley Blunt was born in India in 1859, the daughter of Major-General Charles Harris Blunt (1824-1900), Royal Bengal Artillery, and spent her first 30 years there, alternately in the Punjab & Kashmir. Following the death of her mother in 1892 she and her father returned to England and settled at Halle Place, West Adderbury, where Miss Blunt was an enthusiastic collector of folk song and dance. She died in 1950 and her archive was sent to Cecil Sharp House by Winnie Wyatt, her long-serving maid and companion.

THE FINE COMPANION

"Constant Billy"
see Fyfe, William Hamilton

Fyfe, William Hamilton
William Hamilton Fyfe is the strongest contender to be 'Constant Billy', who is mentioned several times in the Log and makes an appearance at Stratford. There is not quite enough evidence to be absolutely certain, but Fyfe complies with all the known facts. 'Billy' was evidently in Oxford; he is mentioned as partaking of cake at Iffley, and as, like the Vidals, having a dining-table with mats instead of a table-cloth (implying that he was a householder and very probably married); he was a 'first' (i.e. had taken a first-class degree); he greeted the Fine Companions on their arrival in Stratford, later bringing chocolate cake and chocolates, and subsequently a lemon and two pounds of cheese in order to demonstrate how to work the chafing dish. This suggests a certain degree of seniority and indeed affluence. Later he is recorded as gaining his Elementary Certificate. There is also, of course, the probability that his name was William – it would have to be a very recondite reason indeed for 'Constant Billy' to have gained his nickname without being called William.

Fyfe was born in London on 9 July 1878; following his father's early death in 1880 the family were in genteelly impoverished circumstances. Fyfe won a scholarship to Fettes College, Edinburgh, and then one to Merton College, Oxford, where indeed he took a double first class in both classical moderations and in the final school of *literae humaniores*. He then taught at Radley for two years before returning to Merton as a tutor in classics. In 1908 he married Dorothea Hope Geddes White, from Aberdeen; they were to have three children, the elder two of whom were Maurice (born 1909) and Margaret (born 1912); the family lived at 17 Merton Street. Dorothea Fyfe served as treasurer for the Oxford branch of the EFDS, retiring late in 1914.

Fyfe is known to have been a Morris dancer. While serving as Senior Proctor (academic year 1912-13) he took part as a dancer in the Oxford University Dramatic Society production of Dekker's *Shoemaker's Holiday* in February 1913; (See Appendix C). It is even possible that Fyfe, rather than Reg Tiddy, was the 'great man' of the university who took up dancing and was instrumental in bringing about the EFDS branch. He certainly took the chair at the inaugural meeting of the Oxford branch of the EFDS, in place of the President of Magdalen, who had been billed to do so but was unable to be present. (The President of Magdalen at this time was Herbert Warren, 1853-1930, who added interest in the W.E.A., and in women's education, to his nurturing of his college; he is not known to have had a particular interest in folk-dancing, but was undoubtedly a very senior member of the university who would have added weight to the new movement.)

During the Great War Fyfe served in military intelligence; in 1919 he became headmaster of Christ's Hospital, where he revolutionised the curriculum; from 1930 to 1936 he was principal and vice-chancellor of Queen's University, Kingston, Ontario, and from 1936 to 1948 was principal of Aberdeen University. He was knighted in 1942 and died, after a retirement in Blackheath, London, on 13 June 1965.

THE FINE COMPANION

No other candidate for 'Constant Billy' unites all the criteria necessary – name, location in Oxford, first-class degree, good dancer, and the right sort of age and status. His obituary in *The Times* (15 June 1965) remarks that 'he was gifted with a whimsical wit', which matches 'Constant Billy's' funeral service for the Spanish Sausage, so light-heartedly undertaken and so grimly abandoned.

Hampton, Dr.

Probably Frank Anthony Hampton, M.B., Ch.B., 1913, of New College, who served in the R.A.M.C. and was awarded the M.C. He is listed among the Folk Dancers in the Services in the *EFDS Journal* for 1915.

Hawes, Mrs

Katie May Hawes, aged 29, wife of Edmund Thomas Hawes, farmer of the Home Farm at Upton.

Howe, Harold Wilberforce

Mentioned in the Log as an Oxford folk dancer. He was born on 15 Dec 1890, the son of J.F. Howe of Lee, London. He was educated at Eltham College and Merton College, Oxford, where he was a postmaster (scholar) and gained a first in 'Mods' (classics), Hilary 1911, and a second in *Literae Humaniores*, (classics) Trinity 1913; BA 1913, MA 1916.

He was second master at St George's School, Harpenden, 1913-22, served in the Middlesex Regiment 1917-19, returned to teaching and was Headmaster of Keswick School from 1922-46. He was Administrator of Toc H from 1947-51, then went to theological college

(Ripon Hall) and was ordained in 1953, serving as curate of St Margaret's, Addington, Kent, 1953-6 and as vicar St Mary's Woodlands, in the diocese of Rochester, from 1956. He married Margaret Burgess Dell in 1919, had four daughters, and died in 1975 in Tonbridge, Kent.

Although potentially a candidate for being "Constant Billy", he is mentioned in the Log as gaining his Elementary Certificate at the same time as "Billy", which necessarily eliminates him.

DCD pasted a letter from him, dated 1 May 1940, into the *Log*; evidently she had sent it to him to read and he returned it with thanks, but no great indication of previous intimacy; he did not remember 'Alec'.

Jones, Edward Laurence (Teddy, "Rufty")

He was born on 7 August 1891, the son of the Rev. Herbert Edward Jones, later suffragan Bishop of Lewes & Archdeacon of Chichester, and educated at Eton and Balliol College, Oxford, 1911-14, where he became a friend of Alec Hepburne-Scott. He took his BA in 1919 and MA 1928.

By August 1914 he was already engaged to Kathleen Scott, with a wedding planned for 1 March 1914, but, as DCD supposed, this was postponed until 1915. He enlisted with Alec in August 1914 in the London Scottish, but was rapidly invalided out and then worked in the Labour Supply Depot, Ministry of Munitions 1916-17, and in the Ministry of Food, 1917-19. Later he worked in the West Indies & Central America, with the European Cattle Food Supply Co. New Orleans 1920-4, Frank Fehr & Co. Baltic Exchange

1924-6, and the Dunlop Rubber Co. as Continental Inspector 1926, Assistant Export Manager 1927, and as General Manager in Iraq, Persia, India, Burma & Ceylon, 1928-31. In 1931 he retired and travelled in America. In 1932 he became Organizing Secretrary of the Oxford Society, and in 1933 Director of Butterworth & Co, Law Publishers in Australia, in 1935 in India and in London from 1939. He was injured in the Blitz in 1940, being buried by a bomb, but survived to be killed in a motoring accident in 1948.

His first marriage, to Kathleen Nairne Scott of Blackheath, was dissolved in 1922. His second was in to 1923 Mary Senior Williams of Jamaica, and his third, in 1943, to Elinor Wren of Melbourne, Australia; he had no children.

Kennedy, Mr

Mentioned at Stratford. Presumably Douglas Kennedy (1893-1988), Sharp's successor as Director of the EFDS and an early member of the men's morris side. Husband of Helen Karpeles and brother of Helen Kennedy North, 'Madam'; appears in Oxenham's *The Abbey Girls Go Back to School* as 'Joshua'.

Kimber family

'Kimber' is evidently William Kimber the younger (1872-1961), the morris dancer and musician who played the concertina for the morris side who first danced to Cecil Sharp at Headington on Boxing Day 1899 and from whom next day Sharp noted down five tunes. Young Kimber had been taught by his father, 'Old Kimber', who had been a member of the original

Headington Quarry side. In 1905 Sharp sent Mary Neal to 'young' Kimber when she asked him about folk-dances; she brought Kimber to London to teach the girls of the Espérance Club. The interest sparked by this club's dancing stimulated Sharp's own interest in the dance and renewed his contact with Kimber, who transferred loyalty to him, dancing at his demonstrations, contributing new dances to his collections, and training new dancers. DCD must have seen him dance in Oxford on several occasions, but there is no evidence that she had any great contact with him.

Marsh, Ursula

The only Ursula Marsh associated with Epwell was Ursula Alcock, born 1843, who married Richard Marsh in 1867 and died in 1896; in the 1881 Census they were living at the grocer's shop in Epwell, and as Richard Marsh is listed as a farmer it was probably Ursula who was running the shop. DCD appears to have misread the tombstone.

Olive

Oxford folk dancer. Unidentified. Probably not Olive Balls, daughter of the farmer at Yatcombe farm, working locally as a servant, but someone in Oxford.

"Rufty"

see **Jones, Edward Laurence**

Sainsbury, Miss

Beatrice Sainsbury, with Frida Zimmern, was co-proprietor of Boar's Hill Preparatory School, run at

Woodside; she died in Malvern in 1968 aged 92. The school existed by 1911 and was still running in 1915; its later history is not known.

Sidgwick Family

The Sidgwick family, of 64 Woodstock Road, Oxford, were evidently among DCD's closest friends during this period of her life. Mrs Sidgwick was one of the founding members of the EFDS, and was naturally among the founders of the Oxford branch of the EFDS By 1914 she was the branch secretary and we may reasonably assume had been instrumental in bringing DCD to Oxford. From the tone of the *Log of the 'Fine Companion'* we can guess that DCD was a frequent guest at 64 Woodstock Road – it was there, for instance, that she had left her 'Only Other' hat, and the whole family seem to have come to her lodgings at 11 Wood-stock Road to see the van off on its trip to Stratford.

Arthur Sidgwick (1840 – 1920) was one of the sons of the Rev. William Sidgwick, headmaster of Skipton School; one of his brothers was Henry Sidgwick of Cambridge, founder of Newnham College, and his sister was the wife of Archbishop Benson of Canterbury. He himself taught at Rugby and then moved to Oxford to be tutor and fellow of Corpus Christi College, and from 1894-1906 Reader in Greek.

In 1873 he married Charlotte Sophia Wilson; they had five children, among them Ethel (mentioned in the *Log*) who became a novelist and Margaret (Marjorie), who, like her mother, was involved in the folk dance movement; Frank, the elder son, a poet and novelist, founded the publishing firm of Sidgwick and Jackson.

Arthur Sidgwick, a strong Liberal in politics, was a powerful worker in the cause of women's education at Oxford; two of his daughters (Rose and Marjorie) studied history as home students (in the association eventually to become St Anne's College) and Rose became a notable academic.

Charlotte Sidgwick was a clergy daughter from Lincolnshire, some thirteen years her husband's junior. In the summer of 1914 she was sixty, old enough to stand in a quasi-maternal role to DCD. Her obituary in *The Times* (16 May 1924) spoke of 'her entirely individual charm' and maintains

> she was a child of nature, with an instinctive love of the good and the beautiful, which she pursued with a spontaneity and simplicity puzzling to the sophisticated, who mistook her complete lack of self-consciousness for eccentricity ….. She welcomed with delight the revival of folk-music and dancing … There could be no fitter expression for her nature than the naïve and lovely dance, and music of English country folk.

She was involved in the folk-dance revival in Oxford from the beginning (see Appendix C), and, as we have seen, served as secretary for the Oxford branch of the EFDS, resigning the post at the end of 1914 in order to become secretary of the Folk Music subcommittee.

The Sidgwicks lost their younger son, Hugh, in the War; he died on 17 September 1917. Their eldest daughter, Rose, a lecturer in history at Birmingham University, died in the great flu epidemic on 28 December 1918. Arthur Sidgwick died after years of decline on 25

September 1920, and Charlotte in May 1924. Their daughter Ethel, probably the longest survivor of all the people who appear in the *Log of the Fine Companion*, died on 29 April 1970, aged 92.

Sogaard, Ingeborg

Dancer at the London Pavilion who performed at the Cotefield Fête. Nothing further is known of her; she was probably not as well-known as the advertisements made out. The London Pavilion (1885, remodelled 1900) is now called the London Trocadero and is part of the Trocadero Centre, but in its heyday was a music hall de luxe.

Spokes, Edna

Aged 25 in 1914; one of the daughters of George Newcomb Spokes, antique dealer, of Bayworth Corner, Boar's Hill, on the opposite side of the road to The Plain (see **Stevens, C.O.**) and now the site of the Beaumont Nursing Home.

Stevens, Miss C.O.

Catharine Octavia Stevens (1864-1959) was the eighth daughter and youngest of the thirteen children of the Rev. William Stevens, squire and rector of Bradfield, Berkshire, and founder of Bradfield College. Her father's lavish endowment of his project bankrupted him, and he had to leave Bradfield and take a living in Lincolnshire, where C.O.S. (as she liked to be called) acted as his housekeeper. She was twenty-four when he died in 1888; the 1891 census found her in Monken Hadley (only a mile or two from Chipping Barnet, where DCD was then living) and described as a 'student of music', but her real passion was astronomy, which she seems to have taught herself. She was particularly interested in the sun, contributing (for example) articles on various eclipses to the *Journal of the British Astronomical Association*; she had joined the B.A.A. in 1891, the year after its foundation.

Presumably some money had been saved for her from the family wreck, for she was able to visit Algiers, New Zealand, Majorca and later Quebec, and there is no indication that she ever had paid employment. In 1910 she built 'a house-cum-observatory' called The Plain, on Boar's Hill, the site chosen for its observation possibilities, and lived there until 1956. She died three years later at the age of ninety-five, having earned herself the accolade of an obituary in the *Journal of the British Astronomical Association* (Vol.70, no. 1, 1960).

This does not mention any interest in folk-dancing, but that is presumably what introduced her to DCD – unless there had been some much earlier connection when both were resident in Hertfordshire. C.O.S. was of course much older than DCD, but it is not impossible that she had known the Maxwell uncle and aunt. DCD's sister Molly described herself as 'formerly of The Plain' in her marriage particulars, which strengthens the possibility that both girls had known C.O.S in their Barnet days.

The *Fine Companion* was parked in the grounds of The Plain when its log opens, which suggests a reasonably close degree of friendship.

THE FINE COMPANION

Taylor, Miss

Probably Marjorie Taylor of Somerville, see Appendix C.

Vidal family

The Vidal family lived at Windrush, Boar's Hill, very near The Plain. In 1914 the residents were Mrs Vidal, her sons Lance and John and her daughter Lois. Mrs Vidal, born Caroline Elizabeth Andrewes (1852-1932) was the widow of the Rev. Robert Wellington Vidal, Vicar of Bayford, Herts, who had resigned his living in 1902 because of mental health problems and died in Bethlem Hospital on 11 November 1911.

Lance (Lancelot Andrewes, presumably called after the 17th century Bishop of Winchester, but also after his mother's maiden name) had been educated at Malvern and then at Brasenose College, Oxford; from 1909 he had been an assistant master at Radley, only a couple of miles from Boar's Hill, which explains why his mother and sister had moved there. (From 1901 to 1911 the Vidals had lived in Oxford, which suited the children's education.) The younger brother, officially Charles John but apparently always called by his second name, was only nineteen in 1914 and just finished with Marlborough. Their sister Lois was twenty-five and intermittently working as a governess; she was to have a distinctly chequered career (she shared her father's mental instability) and this period at Windrush was probably the happiest of her adult life. Her autobiography, *Magpie: the Autobiography of a Nymph Errant* (1934) gives valuable information about folk-dancing in Oxford and Boar's Hill and about DCD.

Lance Vidal volunteered on the outbreak of war, became a 2nd Lieutenant. in the Oxford and Buckinghamshire Light Infantry (the local regiment) and was killed at Givenchy on 25 September 1915; his name is on the memorial at Loos, showing that, like Alec, he had no known grave.

John Vidal also became a 2nd Lieutenant. in the 'Ox and Bucks', having originally joined up as a private in the Royal Fusiliers, and served in France in 1916. He survived the war, married and had two daughters, and died in 1971.

Not mentioned in the *Log of the Fine Companion* are the elder members of the family, Peter, who had emigrated to Canada, and Dorothy, who had taken a 2nd class in Modern History from the Society of Home Students, Oxford (later St Anne's College); she had a variety of teaching jobs (with more war-related occupations 1914-18), finally at Berkhampstead; she made a late marriage, in 1932, to a widowered cousin, Dr. John Kyffin, and died in 1961.

Three other Vidal children had already died: Mary Theodora, the eldest, at the age of nineteen in 1898; Robert Mark of tubercular blood poisoning in 1900, aged twelve; and Bridget Elizabeth in Canada aged twenty-nine as recently as 29 April 1914. There is no hint in the log of any of the family's tragic background and DCD seems not have been aware of it. She speaks with enthusiasm of the house and its garden, the creation of which Lois describes in *Magpie*.

It was Lance Vidal who introduced the family to folk-dancing, having met it himself at Radley when

THE FINE COMPANION

Cecil Sharp brought a team to demonstrate late in 1913. Lance took Lois to the winter school of folk-dancing at Stratford just after Christmas 1913, and on their return they started the 'Foxcombe Folk Club', enrolling sixty members at the first meeting.

Music was initially provided by John Vidal's clarinet, that of his teacher ('a musical chemist'), and 'a little fiddler from Abingdon'. Later a small piano was bought for ten pounds and installed in the concrete-floored barn where classes were held. Numbers grew, and the club helped to weld together the members of what was still a very new community with no natural centre. It is not clear where the barn was, but it may have been part of the premises of The Plain as DCD describes showing Dr Hampton over the house (i.e. The Plain) and the barn as if they were part of the same property.

Radley College had also taken to dancing (it should be remembered that George Butterworth had been a master there from 1909 to 1910), and Lance and Lois went weekly into Oxford to join DCD's class 'for undergraduates and North Oxford people'.

As soon as war broke out the Folk Club was transformed into a shirt-making session. The Vidals had booked for a fortnight at Stratford, and as Lance could for the moment do nothing (he had a commission in the reserve battalion of the 'Ox and Bucks', but had been instructed to remain in charge of his O.T.C. contingent at Radley, which had in fact disbanded from their camp) they decided to go so that their landlady would not be done out of her fees. This meant that we have Lois

Vidal's testimony for the odd few days at the end of *The Log of the 'Fine Companion'*.

All too soon the household at 'Windrush' broke up, with both sons enlisted and Lois and her mother involved in war-work. The house was sub-let, and given up after Lance's death. The Vidals never returned to Boars Hill.

Lois Vidal at one point worked for the YMCA in France, and says she was instrumental in bringing DCD over to teach folk-dancing. Lance's death seems to have destroyed her stability and she had episodes of mental illness; even when well she was incapable of staying in any job for any length of time, and in the end was estranged even from her mother. Her autobiography ends with her marriage to a naval man, but apparently that did not last either, and the rest of her story is a blank until her death on 28 November 1956.

Watson, William Henry Lowe, D.S.O., D.C.M.

He was born on 3 Aug. 1891, the son of the Rev. Patrick W. Lowe Watson, and educated at Harrow, Göttingen University, Balliol College Oxford (1910-1914), where he was an Exhibitioner and took a second class in Modern History in 1914., being an exact contemporary and friend of 'Alec' He enlisted in 1914 in the Royal Engineers and served as a motor cyclist in France & Belgium, 1914-15, being awarded a DCM on 1 April 1915. He was in the Tank Corps in France from 1916-18, becoming a Major in the 4th battalion and being mentioned in despatches in France 1919; he was awarded the D.S.O. on 3 June 1919.

He became Secretary to the Committee on employment of disabled soldiers in 1919 and passed first into the Civil Service, Ministry of Labour; Principal Clerk 1920. He was Private Secretary to the Minister of Labour from 1928.

He published *Adventures of a Despatch Rider*, 1915, *A Company of Tanks*, 1919, *A Boy's Book of Prose*, 1924, and *Tales from English History* 1925.

He married Ruth Barbara Walker in 1916 and had two sons and a daughter; he died in 1932.

'Wilky'

Mentioned as teaching Morris at Stratford. Probably George J. Wilkinson, one of the first men's morris side of the EFDS.

Zimmern, Miss

Frida Zimmern, born in Manchester of an English mother and German father, was co-proprietor with Beatrice Sainsbury of Boars Hill Preparatory School. She attended Manchester High School and Somerville College, Oxford; she died in Manchester in 1927 aged 50.

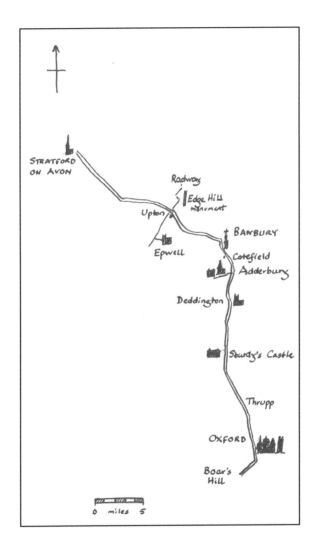

11. The Journey of the 'Fine Companion',
27 July – 1 August 1914

Notes on the Text

DCD's sometimes erratic spelling and punctuation have been retained. There has been some minor reformatting of paragraphs.

The additional 'scrap-book' pages which follow the *Log* have not been included.

Some minor points are elucidated in footnotes. Notes on people whose names are marked * will be found in the section 'People mentioned in the text', pp.55-70.

THE LOG OF THE FINE COMPANION

JULY 23 1914

I came to the Hill Top[1] about 3.0 p.m. The Van was in good order, but needed a clear out, so I saw to that & then bought supplies. The baker was jogging down the road so I stopped his cart. Dorothy gave me tea in the kitchen with her C.O.S.* being at Headington for 'The Dream'[2]. I cleared up everything & then myself, & then rolled round to the Vidals* to ask about the Country Dancing Class. Mrs. Vidal gave me a hearty welcome & the two sons were discovered talking Morris tunes & dances. I was asked to supper, so came back for my shoes & then went into the garden & talked to Lance Vidal. Kimber* told him that old Kimber knows a lot more dances & tunes, but won't tell them to people. The old Headington Side used to be frightfully debauched, & go off at Whitsuntide for weeks & weeks & never come home to their wives. They would be drunk the whole time, & turn up at the end of the trip with no money at all. Then Old Kimber got converted & turned Methodist, so set his face against the Morris. But he had taught all his sons & daughters & they loved it, though he did all he could to discourage it. Young Kimber has taught the Side all he knows, but means to get more out of his father if he can. The old man refuses to speak. Not long ago Old Kimber & Henry Franklin arranged to meet in a pub in Oxford & dance jigs. Young Kimber heard of this, & came down meaning quietly to watch from behind something & see what his father did do – but the old man saw him, & never said a word, but went straight back to Headington without dancing a step. Mr. Vidal says that Young Kimber was a little drunk when he told him this, it must have been pricelessly impressive.

1.   Boar's Hill; near Oxford: this part of it is known as Foxcombe Hill.
2.   Possibly a performance of *A Midsummer Night's Dream*.

12. The Plain, Boar's Hill, 1995

13. Windrush, Boar's Hill, 1995

THE LOG OF THE 'FINE COMPANION'

A gipsy woman once said to Loïs Vidal 'You have a lucky face & a wanting heart.'

We had a nice supper. They have a really fine old oak table & they, like Constant Billy*, don't have any tablecloth, which is delightful. The dancing class was in the school garden. A good many turned up, about eighteen I should think. John Vidal played the clarinet. The dancing was nice, but a few beginners were struggling in the hope of Future Success.

Then I went back to the Van & Dr. Hampton* with me. He brought a Spanish Sausage & a book. He liked the Van.

Then Loïs turned up & I made milk cocoa as there were milk & cream to use up. Spilled the cocoa & then knelt in it. We fetched C.O.S. & she had some too. Then Loïs went, & C.O.S. & I took Dr. Hampton over the house & barn, & then he went home. He left one half a box of cigarettes. He seems to be a kind of supply store – two sprigs of lavender seem a very poor exchange for all this. C.O.S. came & slept in the Van – at least I slept, & she seemed to keep awake, but one always does that one's first night.

July 24

We got up about 6.30 & C.O.S. went to her housework. I put the beds away & then Loïs arrived to breakfast. We had a really nice meal. The Primus was a lamb, but I must not say 'Blast' so often. After breakfast I cycled into Oxford & spent most of the day at 64 Woodstock Rd. writing & packing. I told Mr. Sidgwick* the shwkw [sic] joke, he had never heard it & was vastly pleased. There was a Morris class at 5 o'clock in St. Giles for Miss Taylor*, as she had had no dancing in Rome & was pining for a little before going to Stratford. I got back about 7 o'clock & had a hot bath & took my supper across to C.O.S. The Spanish Sausage is a queer compound, but might grow upon one. We talked Life, & I helped her to wash up. I found Loïs in the dark sitting on the frill. We made our beds & then sat again on the frill till it was too cold.

Then in the Van for tunes on the Accordion, & so to bed. (Pepys)

July 25

We woke early & listened to a lark on the ground getting

77

ready to fly. He made little chirps & twirls of song & then started up & away. I had never heard that before.

Then C.O.S. startled us considerably by hanging over the front door with the letters.

About twenty years ago Mrs. Vidal helped to entertain some London girls from the slums. She asked one her living, & the girl said 'Oh, I'm a Worm Eater.' It appears that she earned her living by drilling holes in faked furniture to look like worm places!

It rained hard, so we shut ourselves in & had a hearty breakfast. Loïs kicked over the coffee pot, so had to wash the floor. Then she went home, & I turned the Van into a laundry & washed clothes. The wind too good to be neglected. Then took my sewing over to the Vidals as they had promised to let me use the sewing machine. Made a nightgown all except the lace & buttonholes. Stayed to lunch. I believe I could be as nice as the Vidals if I lived in a house called 'Windrush' with so many different flowers in the garden.

Came back after lunch & had a visit from Edna Spokes*. We made a chocolate pudding. The blacksmith had been during the morning & painted the new Sharves a bright scarlet. The paint dripping in the sun in all directions & making it a little difficult to get in & out of the Van. One would have thought it a better plan to paint the sharves <u>before</u> putting them on the Van – but I suppose there is a rule about such things. A Blacksmith must know.

A present from Mrs. Vidal of a bunch of mixed herbs & a bag of shalotts from the garden. The herbs hang inside the van, & the shalotts <u>outside</u>. I went over to the Spokes for tea. Edna gave me a very nice paper pattern of a frock for the baby.[1]

Olive* came about seven o'clock with her baggage for the night. We went out together with our jugs & bought milk & cream at the Balls farm. Fred Cooper presented me with a large red dahlia, the first of the season. We carried it in triumph to the Van & were immediately aware of an immense swarm of earwigs. Fortunately they are clean & friendly beasts. The boy at the farm is like nice Mr. Pallet of Kidlington who is such a good Folk Dancer.

Olive immensely pleased with everything – in a voice mounting the octave at every exclamation.

1. Presumably DCD's nephew.

THE LOG OF THE 'FINE COMPANION'

We had scrambled eggs on toast for supper & the chocolate shape with lots of cream, & butter & biscuits, & cocoa made with milk. Olive tried the Spanish Sausage, I felt I could not face it. She said 'are you quite sure that it is <u>good</u>?' & put it down hurridly.

We went to bed early & talked late. The wind was terrific all the night. The Van tugged at her moorings, & when everything rattled there still seemed something left to begin a fresh noise. We were most comfortable. We agreed that there is nothing like the Wind to make one thoroughly understand the comfort of a warm soft bed.

July 26

We waked early & talked & had tunes on the Accordion. 'Shall we gather at the River' because of its being Sunday. Olive read 'Hindle Wakes' breathlessly, & I had 'Time's Laughing Stocks'. One claims 'A Trampwoman's Tragedy' at once. Then we got up without much difficulty. The bath just fits in the Van, & we <u>just</u> fit in the bath!

Breakfast took exactly one hour & a half because we began to discuss Folk Dance Propaganda – this being a subject which one never finishes.

Then Olive went home & I called on C.O.S. in the kitchen. She was stuffing a duck. Our Mag[1] came over & told my fortune with her pack of cards. The most wonderful luck of course but it's the <u>hearing</u> our Mag which is such fun.

Then Miss Zimmern* & her nice German girl called & I showed them the Van, & Edna Spokes came with more paper patterns for the baby. Back to lunch with Miss Zimmern leaving the Spanish Sausage on guard.

A very happy lunch with Miss Sainsbury* there as well. We each told past experiences until we could laugh no more. Cycled to Iffley to see P. about the buying of a dustpan, & then to Cowley to sign legal things for the Baby.

Then to 64 Woodstock Rd. in the pouring rain, my only Hat getting soaked to the skin. Fortunately my Only Other One was at No 64 so I could take that & leave the poor wet thing stretched out to recover. Mr. & Mrs. Sidgwick were alone, so I had tea & we

1. Unidentified. Perhaps a servant at Balls' Farm or The Plain.

talked by the fire. Mr. Sidgwick wrapped in cushions with bad lumbago.

Ethel[1] was in to supper. Then to Sunningwell to see the blacksmith about greasing the wheels, & a screw eye for the luggage carrier behind. he was ready to come & do it at six o'clock in the morning, but that seemed a little early & we arranged a later time. Then a quiet talk in the Van with C.O.S. & then alone on the top rail. A really satisfactory day. Perhaps a little tiring.

July 27

Waked at 6.15 by C.O.S. with an invitation to breakfast. Went over to her & read her some of the Hardy poems. A lordly breakfast in the kitchen side by side. Then back again to pack up the van & wedge all the crockery. A friendly visit from Mr. Ball*, & also Our Mag. The blacksmith's son came at 8.15 to 'look at the luggage carrier', so I sent him back to Sunningwell for a screw eye & his tools. Horse & man came punctually at 8.30. The man very pleasant & a little amused. He just managed to fit the horse into the new sharves. Then to the road to sit & wait for the blacksmith's boy. Waited three quarters of an hour, dancing with impatience to be off & away, but the boy so pleasant when he did arrive that it was impossible to be tart to him.

Then off down the hill. Stopped for supplies in Oxford & baggage from No 11.[2] All the Sidgwicks with P. ready & welcoming. Stacked everything in the Van – showed everybody over her. The man really nice & handy. Then fed by Lilly downstairs as she had overheard the time that breakfast was away, & then off along the Woodstock Rd. We shut ourselves in & packed hard & made all trim – P. pausing suddenly, a little seasick & longing for a walk along the road. Certainly it <u>does</u> heave & shake.

Discovered no sign of my ring. I <u>know</u> I only took it off to get dressed – but missed it just before leaving. It can't be really lost – only mislaid. Perhaps C.O.S. might find it in the grass – it may still be in the Van, but there is no sign – it was Mother's.

Stopped at the Blacksmith's in Summertown to have the wheels greased. Little boys much excited. Packing inside the Van -

1. Sidgwick.
2. DCD's lodgings at 11 Woodstock Road.

& P. on the road. Driver turned round with a grin & said'This is a nice life – ain't it?' Stopped to write it down & suitcase fell off the rail, everything on the floor & fountain pen sneezed over best silk shirt. Fortunately the spots come under the collar. Left our hats inside the Van & walked along the road together. Stopped at the 'Britannia'[1] to feed the horse, & took our lunch over to the canal bank. Bread, bacon, buns, bananas. Drove the horse for a little while. Answers to her helm more than Emma did. Better for the man to drive. The man said that greasing the wheels eased the Van of about half a ton. Horse slipped badly & nearly fell on the smooth tarred road. Exciting. So to 'Sturdy's Castle'[2] by 2.45 p.m. where we found the new horse 'Fanny' waiting by the roadside with a country youth. So out came Captain and back to Oxford with the man & Fanny fitted the sharves & off we went. That strap behind is called the 'breeching' & helps the horse going down hill. The horse sits on it – as it were – & you needn't be frightened if it goes sideways a little because it can get more grip that way.

We had both kinds of couplings put on They Sharves because then we could have a horse with any kind of Harness. There was another boy with a horse named Jolly waiting for us at the foot of Deddington Hill. It is an impossible bit of country for a heavy Van, & the roads are all tarred so there is no foothold for the horses. Our driver said – 'They don't care for the 'osses.' However, the two of them took us up in splendid style. We bought two rolls & some wonderful jam buns at the butcher's shop. We had a meal in the Van, but didn't bother to make any tea. The methylated spirit was slung underneath & the spirit stove seemed stuck together – & after all what's a cup of tea when you are merely hungry?

The second boy sat on Jolly & we went on to Adderbury. Such a welcome from Miss Blunt* & her cousin. We settled into the field & scrubbed out the Van. It needed it after a journey of twenty two miles. We then went into the house where Miss Blunt has the largest bath imaginable. The cook had been coaling up the kitchen fire for hours before our coming. We put on lilac print frocks & brushed our hair. Never could one see or imagine anything more clean than we. Miss Blunt's cousin has collected Indian

1. The Britannia Inn, Thrupp.
2. Inn at the crossroads with the Woodstock-Tackley road.

THE FINE COMPANION

Folk Songs in Kashmir, she sang some after dinner. We looked at the pictures for the Féte tomorrow. There are some lovely things. It was difficult to know how to price them & we couldn't help much there.

14. Adderbury West Manor House
(Le Halle Place)

We went back to the Van at 9.45 p.m. Miss Blunt insisting on our taking the hunting crop with us in case the horses in the field should attack us in the night. She wanted to send us early tea in the morning & a maid to call us at eight o'clock. This we refused – it did not seem to be in the picture. Had a little trial with the hunting crop, but couldn't reach the window from the top rail. Could reach everything else in the Van – including P. – Then settled quietly & read P. to sleep – though she woke up again at 'Pure from the night & splendid for the day' – got soaked to the skin in candle grease. Read myself to sleep. How <u>can</u> people go to fashionable watering places! Owls in the trees in the night – perhaps C.O.S. will find the ring. It is not in the Van – I literally took the Van & shook it upside down but there was no sign of it.

THE LOG OF THE 'FINE COMPANION'

July 28

Waked early both of us, so had time to read. P. deep in with Tagore. No need to hurry, breakfast up at the house being at 9.15. – a most comfortable hour, but hopeless if one had to pack & be on the road by ten o'clock.

P. playing an uncertain 'Jamaica' on the pipe, & then a really recognizable 'Lady Cullen' but stronger on 'Home Sweet Home.' The House is most beautiful. If it were mine I should have all my meals sitting on the staircase. There is a XIV Century stone arch leading to the kitchen. Imagine living there, with ancestors all round the wall with your nose – Mrs. Lawes at Dorchester once was sad to me about the High Church Vicar. She did not approve of early service taken fasting. She said she could not see any reason in it 'The poor stomach has to do the work for all - & if one doesn't come on top – t'other does.'

15. Cotefield House, 1995

P. washed stockings & D. blacked boots. It saves time if one specializes. Then a drive to Cotefield with Miss Blunt, taking our pictures for this afternoon. A happy morning hanging them on screens in the big marquée. It was quite interesting finding out how they should go to show their best. Then back to the house. We passed a motor caravan standing by the roadside – a wonderful modern thing made of three ply. Gentle rain. A hurried lunch. The house is so lovely. Up stairs & down stairs & round corners & always a glimpse which is a sheer delight. Then a quick change into immaculate white, & off to the Fétè with powder on our noses. Mrs. Jones in the village told us that the House is haunted. She mentioned three ghosts. A headless woman, & someone laid in beer in the cellar – but the nicest is 'A rustling lady in the little drawing room.'

The Fétè was fun & had many attractions. I am afraid we were the least of these. There was a Best Baby Prize & an Ugliest Dog Prize (on the terrace) & Bowling for a Pig. We wanted to do this last, but felt it might be embarrassing if we happened to win. The Palmist was a lamb to look upon. Obviously from London, & absolutely IT. D. couldn't help following about – one understands young men. The county there in force. But how foolish some looked. Tags & ends of materials tied together round the middle with something different – & some of them such really lovely young women. Why do they?

Ingeborg Sogaard* danced to Grieg behind a fence, but we couldn't go & see her because we were selling pictures. We really did enjoy ourselves – but it was amazingly hard work – & dear Miss Blunt began to look so tired, but couldn't rest because she knew everyone who wandered in. We made small purchases. A large bunch of lavender & the two little Kashmir drawings, & P. succumbed to the Malta sketches.

Then we packed up & fell into the carriage, & so back again – So dog tired that it seemed absurd – far more tired than after a long day's trek. One only felt fit to crawl onto the top rail & blow out the candle. A quiet slow dinner. Miss Blunt told us about Miss Meta Brown who lives in Scotland and is a healer. She believes in the healing power of colours, & makes her patients wear clothes of their own influencing shade – which sounds entirely foolish written down like this but not at all so as told by Miss Blunt. Then P. played the Bechstein. She is wonderful. Then a hot bath & back to the Van. Too tired for anything but silence. If P. had talked much D. would have snapped, but fortunately she hardly said a word, so it was just possible to maintain an attitude of melancholy affection.

July 29

We tumbled up fairly early & packed everything. It did not take long as things are now so ship shape that we know our space to the inch. Poor Miss Blunt so tired at breakfast time after her hard day yesterday. She asked me to copy my record of the Endless One so that she may send it to Miss Meta Brown who is interested in charms & amulets. The maids from the House to see the Van. Overcome with admiration – the household arrangements appealing to their expert minds.

Then came a man with – to our horror – <u>two</u> horses. We felt that we were face to face with utter ruin. What could we do? We held our breath & asked his charge, it was no more for one horse than for two – he would charge us 10/6 for the fourteen miles, & having an extra horse he had brought him along to save the other on the hilly road.

How grand we shall feel all the day. I wonder if I could sit on the front one & go along like that.

A nice man with a smile – he said ''tis a roomy Van – 'tis deceivin'.'

Miss Blunt gave us lettuces & some sections of honey. She walked with us through the village & so waved goodbye. We were sorry to leave her.

D. cycled into Banbury to buy supplies – the food shops there are most excellent. The Van waited by the Cross[1] till we had finished, & stowed the purchases away in the locker behind.

The man has brought a little boy with him whose duty it is to sit on the frill & hold the reins while the man leads the horses. The little boy very silent – he seemed a little puzzled at the piece of chocolate, but eventually knew what to do with it.

The road goes steadily up hill to Edge Hill. The cornfields are wonderful. Mr. Dealy – our driver – told us that it is the best harvest we have had since 1898.

---

1. Banbury Cross, erected to commemorate the marriage of the Princess Royal to Prince Frederick William of Prussia in 1859.

THE FINE COMPANION

The back horse is named Dapple & the Front one Ben. D. sat on Ben for about three miles – it was splendid – & so funny to feel his skin twitching under one's ankle.

Mr. Dealy was vastly amused & warned about stiffness – but he doesn't know our Morris legs.

Then a halt at the 'Hare & Hounds' & a happy lunch on the Van. P. went for milk but they had none – we had imagined coffee – so we had Cider instead. Mr. Dealy refused this, being a teetotaler – but he & Fred accepted each a jam bun to sweeten their sandwiches.

P. astride Ben & D. peeling mushrooms in the Van – the view becoming more & more magnificent. Then through to Upton. D. on Ben – to the Home Farm. The farmer[1] pleased to have us in the field only we must go where the hay had been cleared & not where it is just cut.

We pitched near the cottage with our back to a row of elm-trees. Goodbye to Mr. Dealy who wished us a happy holiday. Tea in no time. There was only skim milk at the farm so we said we would wait for the new milking – & in the meantime the kettle boiled so we had Russian tea instead. N.B. <u>Always</u> carry lemons. Tea on the grass by the Van, the sun shining. Iffley cake is wonderful. There arrived a small boy with a jug of the new milk – the bluest eyes possible – & the worst possible squint.

P. pitched the tent. D. made a pudding out of the stale buns & one egg. If only one had vanilla essence – but the only flavouring in the locker is anchovy. Aha! the lemon of course – & some jam. Lord only knows how it will taste – but it looks extremely nice in the bowl Aunt Mary gave us.

Then more cooking – in fact, D. cooked everything she lay her hands upon. Then hot baths in the tent. Then stripped some of the lavender for bags. Then supper. The little Duck [? Dutch] oven is a real lamb. You put things in it for a real long time [,] you leave it alone, & then P. says you are a most wonderful cook.

We had just finished supper & had eaten absolutely everything, when P. gave a shout & leaped from the tent. D. looked, & there was Alec with a cycle coming from the wrong corner of the field, & looking as if he had just dropped in for a friendly call on

---

1. E.T. Hawes, see section on People in the *Log*.

86

his way along the road. D. shouted then, & everybody fell into everybody else's arms. Then to feed him. Started with scrambled eggs but they seemed inadequate to support that frame, so dug some sausages (English) out of the locker & fried them. The sausages were a little sudden in their behaviour & spread out into crumbs in the most horrifying manner, but Alec seemed satisfied.

We had said before leaving – quite casually that we should be through Banbury on Wednesday.

Alec staing [sic] in Oxford with William Watson*, sent him on a Motor Cycle to Banbury to tell us to wait – but the cycle broke down three miles out of Banbury. William Watson telegraphed to Alec, who caught the next train. In Banbury he hired a cycle & tracked us along the road – one man said a 'menagerie' had gone by that way, & another remembered our name 'The Fine Companion'. Once he lost us entirely & had to go back again for miles. Then coffee in the tent – & gossip. Sheep in the distance, a barking dog, & owls, & the little singing of the silent Primus in the Van, & Alec puffing a cigarette.

We didn't bother to tell our adventures, but just handed our logs to him. He says they will always be nice to read, even when we are dying. Then we turned the tent into a really nice bedroom for him, with one of the spring beds & a camp washstand & a chair & a little lamp. Then we washed up & boiled kettles to wash ourselves, & sat on the frill & drank Horlick [sic] & said goodnight to Alec & turned in.

Alec was polite over the Horlick but said it reminded him a little of mumps[1].

And so to bed. P. in a wild paroxysm of terror because she said a black beetle with two tails had suddenly settled on her log. Probably her Horlick was a little too strong, for she is not usually given to romancing.

July 30

Read Border Ballads to P. while she was dressing. She was overcome by one or two of them. And they are bloody. Alec went to the farm for eggs – one wonders what the farmer's wife thought

1. Alec had had mumps at Oxford in March 1914.

of him – she must have thought that we had curiously changed during the night! A happy breakfast with the sun shining & a little wind. Disgracefully late – 9 o'clock or so.

Alec to the Village in search of a carrier to take his hired cycle back to Banbury.

The woman at the cottage says that she lived in a caravan for fifteen years selling Banbury Cakes all round Leamington & Stratford. That was when her first husband was alive 'tis her second husband that she has now. There are marigolds in the garden. Why are marigolds so neglected, except in cottage gardens? One would always have a clump of them in the sun where a wall makes a corner. P. making Alec's bed found fifteen earwigs. Then the three of us with packed lunch basket, books & needlework off to find the village.

There was a short cut through a cornfield. A little path of red earth about a foot wide through the corn, which brushed one's face as we walked, poppies & scabious & billy buttons & little blue birds eye as the edges thinned. Such a road afterwards with every kind of flower. Pale scabious & a deeper coloured thistle in clumps behind & then clover & yellow bedstraw.

So to the Castle Inn[1], & a man said we could go down the steps to the valley. So through the trees down the hill. There was a monument[2] at the bottom, but only about the Battle of Waterloo. We have a better one at home[3].

THE EARL OF WARWICK DEFEATED AND SLAIN.
Stick no Bills.

The path seemed to lead to a big house, & no where else, so we felt doubtful. Alec put on his Best Manner & we got ready to smile & explain. We could always say that we had bought the eggs. Then we found that the path went past the house, so probably the village would soon be found. A Church Spire was poking out from the trees. Then a rest under a big elm tree to write up our logs & look at the 'vista', I think that is the proper word

1. At Edgehill.
2. Erected 1854.
3. At Monken Hadley, commemorating the battle of Barnet, 1471.

THE LOG OF THE 'FINE COMPANION'

People say that Two is Company – but Three can be more delight-ful than anything – only it is much more difficult to find a right Three. That's the real truth, while two will nearly always shake down & be happy.

There was a man on the road. He said that there is no shop, but that they might let us have a loaf of bread at the cottage where the tree is. So we marched to the cottage. A long low whitewashed kitchen with a half door, & a woman inside ironing, & a little boy having dinner at the table. She brought a loaf of baker's bread from an inner room & we paid for it, & then caught sight of a just cut loaf of home-made on the table. We asked her to exchange – to keep the baker's loaf & let us have hers; she thought us a little queer, but we smiled steadily at her & she did what we wanted. We also bought a bottle of cherry cider & a bottle of lemonade, but proper cider at at pub is more satisfactory – only there is no pub here. She says the Village is called Radway. Then along the road & past a little Tudor cottage with a corner in the garden – one could make a Home of that.

There was a field of new cut hay, so we jumped over a gate & settled under a big tree for lunch. Lettuce, home made bread, & butter from the farm. Cheese – honey – rasin [sic] cake. Peace.

P. suddenly said this:-

There once was an Ichysaurus –
Who lived when the Earth was quite porous:
When he first heard his name
He fainted with shame
And departed long ages before us.

A long lazy afternoon with books & needle. P. sang German songs & read Turgenev to us. Alec slept. D. made lavender bags. Then a reluctant packing & back to the road.

Can <u>anyone</u> spell this? 'Outside a cemetary stood a harassed pedlar & an embarrassed cobbler guaging the symmmetry of a lady's ankle with unparalled [sic] ecstasy.' D. made seven mis-takes, & later on – when we asked him – even Constant Billy* made one, & he's a First.

Then a long stiff hill, but we trudged on till we came to the top. A motor passed us. It was standing there when we struggled up, & the lady asked us the way to Cirencester. We suggested all kinds of ways & Alec offered a map, but the man said they had one. We said a few sentences to the lady & then went on. It struck us that she had asked us in order to find out what kind we are - & certainly we do look tramps: we congratulated each other, that at any rate our accents are alright.

Back through our cornfield & D. to the farm for milk & cream. Such a welcome from kind Mrs. Hawes*. P. & Alec had been to the farm the other times. Back to the Van to find tea all ready on the table. The Iffley soda cake again – the kind that William Watson* liked that Sunday on the river. He said – 'I could kiss this cake!' Alec is a wonderful young man. There he is quietly putting away things without anybody telling him. D. with her usual clumsiness knocked over the cream & had to go to the farm for more. Mrs. Hawes said 'Yes, it is serious, but accidents do happen – even indoors.'

After supper the sky looked grim, so we washed up in a great hurry & put everything under cover, Alec pinning down the little frill round the top of his tent so that no rain could blow in. Then a little quiet shower, so we three in the Van, P. & Alec writing logs & D. concocting tomorrow's breakfast. We had felt a sudden craving for mushrooms & asked advice at the cottage. A girl went into the fields & came back in a little while with a heaped plateful. She asked 4^d. The Spanish sausage is getting on my nerves. No one will eat it. P. was most decided: she said 'My God – it's a Blutwurst.' Something must be done with it because it is so obviously nourishing.

The rain again, & reading 'Peacock Pie' to P.

11.5 p.m. P. says 'Mother won't know.'

July 31

I will not go to Stratford today – I will not. This pitch is too lovely to leave & the day is too beautiful. If we start at eight o'clock tomorrow I am certain we could get to Stratford & fix camp by the evening. Alec shall tell the farmer when he goes for the milk. P. says it may rain tomorrow & that would delay us – but if it does rain, we can only get wet, & Alec will work like a horse. We shouted to Alec & he said we would stay. Read Border Ballads to P. Some of them are terrible. It makes one feel a little frightened of Alec, he's Scotch. Suppose he burnt the Van in the night with us in it!

Breakfast – then D. cycled to the village for supplies for dinner tonight. It is quite easy to feed a Man. Apparently he takes the same kind of food as a woman, only you must be careful to leave much more than you think necessary in the bottom of the saucepan for him to have another helping.

A man came into the field with a little cart. He stopped at the cottage & we went to see what was in it. Articles as follows:– Cucumbers oil lemons darning wool candles soap bootlaces. Pins scrubbing brushes rabbit food. Starch boot blacking soda metal polish. Tape cottons brushes writing paper. Bananas with picture postcards. Tomatoes plums tea. Foot rules. Suspender elastic. Sandpaper cocoa laundry blue. Safety pins. Nail brushes matches 'Zam Buk' jam covers. Tin tacks luggage labels boot laces. His name is J.H. Townsend. Middle Tysoe. General Dealer - & he has a hat of the same make as Alec's.

Then off along the road to see Compton Wyniates. P. & Alec walking, & D. on Norah Jones with the baggage strapped behind. Beds of purple veitch [sic] by the road side – yellow scotch daisies, poppies wild antirhinum [sic] – betony & ever so many more.

Coming to Epwell White House we found that Compton is still two miles away, so seeing a wood we decided to stay there. A woman at the cottage said that there is no where to get anything to drink nearer than Epwell – so – the Family being Terrible thirsty, D. on Norah Jones to the public house about a mile & a half away. A most curious village: so dead & forsaken & quaint. All the houses built of a stone brown & green with moss, & put at any angle to the road. The Chandlers' Arms was the Public House, & the gentleman & his wife were very kind. They had no cider, but offered ginger wine – however D. bought Stone Ginger instead as P. is non alcoholic except for cider away from home & out of doors.

The gentleman says that it is a funny place – the people don't care for anything – the houses are never repaired & the land let to go to rack & ruin. That old burnt down house by the Church used to be a monastery, & they say that there was once an underground passage from it to the Church. The lady tied the Ginger Beer bottles together with a string, so that D. could sling them round her neck like milking pails.

16. Epwell Church, 1995

The Church looked so little & quaint that it was impossible to pass it by, so the bottles were put on a grave as it seemed rude to take them inside. Such a little crude old Church – Early English with the queerest shaped arch. There was a man painting the door, so D. borrowed a pencil to put it down. The man sharpened it most beautifully first, with an enormous chisel.

The arch wider at the top than at the bottom.
The two sides of the arch are alike in the original.)

17. Epwell Church, interior, 1995

THE LOG OF THE 'FINE COMPANION'

A dear little carved cross in the Churchyard with sprays of little stone roses. 'In memory of Ursula Marsh'.* She died in 1843. She must have been nice with a name like that, & they must have loved her to have given her afterwards such a pretty little cross.

Then back to the wood, a most glorious place with bracken & piles of brown brushwood & P. said 'Wild raspberries.'

<u>Such</u> a lunch! P. said 'Oh yes, probably a XIV Century ogee arch.' So D. needn't have been so excited.

A long lazy afternoon & D. back to the Van to cook dinner, Alec & P. walking to Epwell to return the bottles. D. put on the Irish stew which always takes hours & hours to cook, & then P. arrived alone, Alec having gone on to the Village to post letters. P. refused tea – said she didn't want any – but fairly wolfed the bread & honey when it was put before her.

No Alec – where could he be? He wouldn't have had time to be drunk by the roadside – would he? & far more serious – <u>no</u> <u>butter</u>! So D. on Norah to the village. Alec was met trudging back along the road, & D. said 'My dear, have you had any food?' Alec said 'Well I was hungry, so I bought a pennyworth of acid drops' & showed the bag! Too much for them both & D. fell off the cycle & knocked Alec's arm & the acid drops were scattered on the high road. However they both picked them up & polished them on their trousers & went their separate ways munching.

There was a wonderful smell of new pastry in the village shop, so D. asked if it could be jam tarts? Miss Fox said she had just taken some out of the oven, so D. demanded them. Miss Fox said – 'Well come into the kitchen & look at them!' so into the kitchen, & there they were all hot in their little pans. D. said 'Two dozen,' & seized a knife & so did Miss Fox & they were soon out of their pans & in a box. The children <u>were</u> so pleased & had two each at once when the box was opened. This log is all about food, but that is because it is being kept by the Cook.

Primus had hysterics & the big kettle fell over – – – There is a little rain & the big black slugs are crawling out on the road. D. remembers, when she was young, picking up one of these thinking it to be a nice umbrella tassel.

To have a hot bath out in a field at ten o'clock at night – & to dance about in your slippers under a big tree!! Milk cocoa.

THE FINE COMPANION

August 1

A happy month to us all. The rain was coming down steadily at 6.0 pm [sic] when P. sternly shouted that people must <u>get up</u>. Then a scramble & real hard work. Alec & P. outside with the tent D. inside stacking beds & then cooking breakfast. D. to the farm for milk, she having indiarubber wellingtons which made it possible to walk through the acre of newly cut hay. A hearty breakfast in the Van & then to clear away & wash up & wedge everything for the journey. Not quite ready when the horse came at 8 o'clock, but soon off along the road.

D. with cycle trundled to the farm to say goodbye to Mrs. Hawes. D. said fervently 'Please God we would come again next year –' & Mrs Hawes said 'Well, ye can have the same horse & the same yung feller.'

Then Sunrising Hill to come down, one of the worst possible places. 1 in 5 & curves & windings all the way. Yesterday, when going to Epwell, a man said there were no hills on the road, but several 'banks'– & though the road turned out to be a veritable switch back we realized the true meaning of 'hill' when we came to Sun Rising. The cottage women tell of accidents that have happened at one time or another at every curve. We saw the orchard where the traction engine crashed, carrying behind it menagerie Vans full of wild beasts – & we identified the telegraph post where 'the young man's brains was found.'!

However, the Fine Companion came down safely, but with a tremendous shaking that shook apart a beam in front, & made the front door impossible to open - & then impossible to shut. D. could not bear the thought of all the precious food getting jolted & spilt & stuck together, so put up her feet & coasted down to the foot of the hill & sat on a gate & wrote up her log. Sat so quietly that a little field mouse came out & played about on the earth at the foot of the gate – D. watching till the most awful pins & needles developed in both feet.

Rain – rain – dripping trees & wet grass & no horizon; the weather clearing a little later on, but still very damp. After a steady nine miles, the horse setting the pace at four miles an hour, a, for the walkers, very welcome halt by the roadside for lunch. Then D. cycled on into Stratford to get the gate opened & at the bridge met

THE LOG OF THE 'FINE COMPANION'

Constant Billy* cycling to meet the Family. Back together to interview Mr. Brown – round to the School for letters & then to meet the Van. Dear me – how <u>nice</u>,

Then a very busy afternoon. Alec & P. putting up tents & D. scrubbing inside. Billy on the frill reading this log – he said 'I shall publish it.' Just time to jump into gym tunics & hot baths & then to tea with Bill in the lovely garden where he is. Then to the school & everybodys bosom & then a class with Wilky* to teach it. Then on Norah Jones to shop for Sunday, getting so wet.

Then back again & into dry clothes & dinner to cook. Alec came to dinner & Billy rolled round afterwards bringing a chocolate cake & chocolates. He thinking us to be poor forlorn creatures with nothing nice around us. A hearty meal in the tent. Billy went out & bought a lemon squeezer & made some drink & also some cheese to show us how to work Lilian who is the chafing dish. He bought two pounds of cheese! Then P. to interview the Chief[1] & we others washing up. A friendly visit from Miss Roberts & three of the Scarborough contingent. They all pleased to see the Van. The whole party turned out by D. at 9.45. Then arrived a weary P. to her tent & then only a screech owl in the trees.

Sunday, August 2

A very wet morning but a happy late breakfast in the Van – with hearty rejoicings at its watertightness & the dryness of the big A.tent. Then chores unending & dinner put on the stoves. P. in thick coat & boots round & about outside. Then head washings & dryings & combings. Then the awful discovery of rain coming into the Van in two places. D. hurridly into a short gym suit & oilskins & sou'wester & a difficult clamber on to the roof of the van. The rain pelting. The only thing to do was to sprawl on one's face & untie the Willesden canvas from over the luggage rail & spread it on the top of the Van holding it in place with carpet nails. It was an exciting job – because the wind siezed [sic] the canvas which attacked D. & knocked her down – v. wetting in spite of waterproof clothing. Then a clamber down & a change almost to the skin. P. replaced the ladder most carefully, D. got out of the Van & the ladder gave way & there was a most wonderful crash. Result a really fine bruise which came on the top of an egg shaped bump. If it had only been on the

1. Presumably Cecil Sharp*.

nose instead of the right shin, everyone would have noticed it & been sorry. Then dinner. Then Billy & Alec to coffee & a long afternoon of reading sewing letter writing & heart to hearters. The Salvation Army providing music round the corner: D. saying 'That's to the Glory of God – they don't make a noise like that to anyone else.'

A letter from C.O.S. saying that the ring is found. It was discovered by Our Mag – in the grass. Oh dear. How <u>satisfying</u>.

August 3

This afternoon a telegram from Rufty* saying [cancelled, ? war has been declared that] – that there is fighting on the North Sea, & asking Alec to meet him in London tomorrow so that they can enlist together. Alec is going, but has telegraphed to his father as he may want him to be with him. P. & D. writing to Rufty. There may be some work for us. We are strong & cheerful & can cook – though God knows that it is very little to be able to do.

August 4

A happy day. Billy writing the funeral service of the Spanish sausage all afternoon. For the procession – a recipe – intoned Gregorian tune. The response – 'Cheer up, the wurst is yet to come.' Alec to come to supper for some of his favourite sausage stew, & mushrooms. D. teaching in evening school.

Alec arrived early with a telegram from London. He is to go tonight & enlist, they may be off at any minute. There wasn't time for any supper. P. went to the station to say goodbye. D. didn't go, because one was enough, & besides, he may never come back – & one doesn't have scenes.

August 5

War was declared last evening. D. bought some lentils etc. this morning. They were 2/- instead of 1/4. Everything has gone up 1^d per pound, but that is just a scare & because of the sudden rush & will settle down later.

Mr. Sharp* has decided to carry on the School as long as possible, it is silly to disorganize things. We shall have the funeral just the same. Mr. Kennedy* says he will be the undertaker instead of Alec.

THE LOG OF THE 'FINE COMPANION'

Telegram from Alec. Daking, Girdlestone. Paddock. Western Lane Stratford on Avon. Rufty* & I enlist London Scottish tonight. Love. Alec.

The baker is in trouble because they have taken his horses to help get the Yeomanry away today, & he cannot deliver on this Country Round. Billy* came to supper. He washed up & put away all by himself. He did it most beautifully & even washed the cloth out afterwards & hung it up in the right place. He must be the only First who can do a thing like that really well.

D. went to the Town Hall to volunteer for emergency duty. She said she understands camping & can cook & sew. She looked as competent as possible. The men were very nice indeed, & said there would be something.

The Funeral of the Spanish Sausage is abandoned. With the sudden rise in the price of food it seems foolish to destroy an article which may be so needed later on.

P. packing Alec's things to send after him. Not a pair of socks or a shirt in decent repair – such darning & button sewing, but he will be comfortable for a bit, at any rate. After going to bed, there was a visit from Mrs. Brown. She came to say that some German ships have been sunk & that Japan is ready to help. We shall need everybody.

August 6

We went to the Town Hall together, as P. had the brilliant idea that if we could be bracketed we'd be able to take the A tent & two beds & a small outfit, & be put down anywhere where needed. P. learning to cook. We explained that we could be jolly useful. Benson was entering his name at the same time.

D. taught the Flamborough in morning school. A class of raw beginners in long tight skirts & corsets poor lambs, but intelligent & even affectionate.

Billy* & Mr. Howe* both passed their elementary examinations last evening. Letters from Alec & Rufty* – they have both signed on for four years. Poor K. She & Rufty won't be married on March 1 now.

D. came in late at night from a walk, & sat down on a basin of soup.

97

THE FINE COMPANION

*   *   *   *   *

November 28

A letter from Alec. He has been for eleven days & nights in the trenches at Ypres & is now off duty for a little rest. He has not been hit – so far – but is having to go to the Doctor every day.

And we at home knit & knit, & welcome those poor Belgians & try in some way to help in all this nightmare of so terribly altered social conditions.

And all those boys out there – seeing Death like that – the Death that is not <u>laid out</u> ………..

Perhaps this is a Dream, & all the before was true – or was <u>that</u> the Dream. They cannot both be true – at least not in the same year?

*   *   *   *   *

Alec was killed in the Ypres sector early in 1915.

I had a little note, written in pencil on a leaf from a note-book. He said "We are just going into action. It is all so beastly that it must be for some good purpose."

It was his last remark, for he was killed that night.

I sent the note to his mother.

APPENDIX A

BOOKS READ OR MENTIONED IN THE *LOG*

Border Ballads, 30 July.
> Presumably an anthology. It is worth noting that the third series (1906) of Frank Sidgwick's *Popular Ballads of the Olden Time* (1903-12) was devoted to *Ballads of Scottish Traditional Romance*

de la Mare, Walter, *Peacock Pie* (1913), 30 July

Hardy, Thomas, *Time's Laughing Stocks* (1909), 26 July
> *Poems*, 27 July

Houghton, Stanley, *Hindle Wakes* (1912), 26 July
> (read by Olive)

Meredith, George, quotation 'Pure from the night & splendid for the day') from *Love in the Valley*, 27 July

Tagore, Rabinadrath, 28 July
> No indication of which work of Tagore, but possibly *Gitanjali: Song Offering* (1912). The poet had been awarded the Nobel Prize for Literature in 1913.

IN AID OF THE HORTON INFIRMARY, BANBURY.

A

GARDEN FETE

Organised by the Girls' Diocesan Association, will be held,
by kind permission of Leigh Hoskyns, Esq., at

COTEFIELD

Two Miles from Banbury, on

TUESDAY, JULY 28, 1914

THE MAYORESS OF BANBURY has very kindly
consented to Open the Fete.

Among the many attractions are—

CONCERT,

With Miss GRACE HOSKYNS, the Celebrated Dancer from
the London Pavilion—INGEBORG SOGAARD;

GREAT BALLOON CONTEST. TREASURE HUNT.

BABY SHOW. CHILDREN'S SPORTS.

DOG COMPETITION, Ugliest Dog Wins.
Numerous other Side Shows.

BAND. TEA & LIGHT REFRESHMENTS.

DANCING —Fancy Dress Competitions in the Evening

For further particulars of Competitions see handbills.

GATE OPENED 2.30 p.m. ENTRANCE 1/- 6d. after
5 o'clock.

THE ENTERTAINMENTS WILL BE REPEATED
IN THE EVENING.

Advertisement for the Cotefield Fete in *The Banbury Guardian*, 23 July 1914

100

APPENDIX B

THE COTEFIELD FÊTE

THE garden party attended by the Fine Companions on 28 July 1914 was held at Cotefield House near Banbury, the residence of the Hoskyns family. It was, and is, a large late 19th century house (the date over the porch is 1904, but the main house is 1870), holding (according to the 1911 census) 26 rooms including the kitchen but excluding scullery, landing, lobby, closet, and bathrooms – more than adequate, one imagines, for Mr Leigh Hoskyns, his wife, two unmarried daughters and son, together with an appropriate number of servants (8 in 1911, excluding outdoor staff).

Only a week before the occasion the plans for the whole fête must have been put in jeopardy, not by the usual doubts about the weather but by the death on 22 July of Leigh Hoskyns' elder brother, Sir Chandos Hoskyns, who left only three daughters; the strict mourning protocol of the age prevented the new baronet and his wife from attending the festivities in their own garden, but permitted their two younger daughters, Frances and Catherine, aged about 27 and 25, to act as hostesses. Also lost to the occasion was Miss Grace Hoskyns, who should have taken part in the concert. She was doubly related to the dead baronet because she was not only his niece but also, through her mother, of the newly widowed Lady Hoskyns.

Rising to the occasion, however, was General Henry Bowles, the new Lady Hoskyns' brother. No doubt military life had accustomed him to coping with emergencies, and he gallantly filled in for Sir Leigh in welcoming the Mayoress of Banbury and then took a vocal part in the two concerts. The Mildred Bowles who performed on the piano was his unmarried sister, in her middle forties, and the Captain Bowles, R.N., who was recorded by the assiduous *Banbury Guardian* reporter as present, was his younger brother – no doubt Cotefield House was roomy enough to house them all for the weekend.

THE FINE COMPANION

Leigh Hoskyns was the third of the six sons of the Rev. Sir John Leigh Hoskyns, 9th baronet, rector of Aston Tirrold, Berkshire, who had died only three years earlier at the age of 92, outliving his eldest son. The second son, Sir Chandos, left only daughters, and because Sir Leigh's only son, a professional soldier, was killed in France on 21 October 1914, it was ultimately the fourth son, the Right Rev. Edwyn Hoskyns, Bishop of Southwell, who inherited the title and passed it on to his son. The fifth brother, Peyton, had entered the Royal Navy (becoming an admiral), and the sixth, Benedict, like his elder brother, the church; he became an archdeacon. The six Hoskyns brothers, in fact, neatly illustrate the careers open to late Victorian gentlemen, as the two elder sons both served in the army.

Leigh Hoskyns had been called to the bar in 1875 and served as Crown Prosecutor of Griqualand West from 1880 to 1885, after which he settled in Oxfordshire, buying Cotefield in 1894. This early retirement (he was 35) appears to have been possible because he made the most of his South African opportunities – Griqualand West centres on Kimberley, where the diamond mines were just getting under way, and Leigh Hoskyns also appears as director of the Consolidated Goldfields of South Africa, one of Cecil Rhodes' ventures. The inescapable conclusion is that he had made a handsome fortune and was henceforth able to live the life of a country gentleman. He and his wife, born Frances Bowles, had four children: three daughters (one already married in 1914) and a son, a twenty-four-year-old soldier who had three months more of life. Sir Leigh had served as High Sheriff of Oxfordshire and was a magistrate; Lady Hoskyns interested herself in the Girls' Friendly Society, and no doubt it was under her auspices that the Horton Infirmary garden fête was held at Cotefield.

The *Banbury Guardian* duly carried a full account of the event the following week (30 July):

FETE IN AID OF THE HORTON INFIRMARY

SUCCESSFUL GATHERING AT COTEFIELD HOUSE OPENING BY THE MAYORESS OF BANBURY

THE COTEFIELD FETE

A large and representative gathering of visitors from Banbury and the neighbourhood were present at a garden fete organised by the girls of the Diocesan Association, by kind permission of Sir Leigh and Lady Hoskyns, at Cotefield, on Tuesday, and which was opened by the Mayoress of Banbury (Mrs. A.J. Larkin Smith), who was accompanied by the Mayor. Owing to the recent death of Sir Chandos Hoskyns, Sir Leigh and Lady Hoskyns could not be present to take part in the proceedings, the Misses Hoskyns being the hostesses for the day. Amongst the leading people attending were General Bowles, Captain Bowles, R.N., Miss Bowles, Mrs. and Miss Blacklock, Mr. Blacklock, Jun., Mrs. E. Slater Harrison, Miss Perry, Mrs. Waldron, Mrs. Thorne, Miss Blunt, Miss Dodgson, Miss North, the Misses Fitzgerald, Miss Starkey, Captain and Mrs. and Miss Paul, Mr & Mrs. Ridley Thompson, Captain and Mrs. Yates, Miss Morrell, Mrs. Roger North, Miss Ommanney and Miss Chipperfield, Mr G. Norris, the Misses Page (Banbury), Miss Rothe, Mrs. and the Misses Pemberton and Miss Barford, Dr. and Mrs. Penrose, Mr and Miss Fisher, the Rev. C.F. and Mrs. Cholmondeley, Mrs. B.N. Ogle, Dr Francy, Miss Margaret Brown, the Misses Wykham Martin, the Misses Cawley, the Rev. and Mrs. Morgan, Miss Hartley, Mr. L.W. Stone, the Rev. Vander Kallen, Mrs. F.J. Dalby and Miss Bowen, Dr. Pritchard, the Rev. C.J. Shebbeare, Mrs. and Miss Holbech, Mr W.C. Hurley, Mr H.W. Stilgoe, Miss Dorothy Willes, Miss Kenworthy, Miss Blagden, and many others. Dr. Faulkner was unavoidably prevented from attending.

The opening ceremony took place on the terrace, the Mayoress being presented by Miss K. Hoskyns with a bouquet of roses, which had been given by the firm of P.J. Perry.

General Bowles, in introducing the Mayoress to the assembly, said he had to explain that owing to the very recent death of his brother, Mr Leigh Hoskyns was quite unable to be present that day, much to his regret, but he felt it was undesirable and quite unnecessary to postpone the fete on account of a family bereavement when all the arrangements had been made. The fete had been organised by the Girls' Diocesan Association for a charitable purpose. One of the objects of that Association was to do good to others by personal service, and they intended to devote the proceeds of that fete to the Horton Infirmary at Banbury.

THE FINE COMPANION

As everyone in that neighbourhood knew, that was a most deserving and excellent instititution, and just now, always, he believed, it was in want of funds to extend the scope of its usefulness. He would ask the Mayoress to declare the fete open.

The MAYORESS, who was well received, said she had the greatest pleasure in declaring the fete open, and she wished it every possible success (applause).

The attractions of the fete then commenced, and there was much to divert one's attention. There was a concert in the hall, when the following programme was performed in an admirable manner, there being a large attendance: "Meine Liebe ist Grün (Brahms) and "Traum durch die Dämmerung" (Strauss), Miss Mildred Bowles; pianoforte solo, Mrs. Slater Harrison; "Ich wand'le unter Blumen" (Meyer Helmund), "Allnächlich im Traume" (Schumann), "At Dawning" (Cadman), "The Ladies of St. James'" (Clarke), "If All the Young Maidens" (Hermann Löhr), General Bowles; pianoforte solo, Mrs. Slater Harrison; "The Infinite Shining Heavens" (Vaughan Williams), "The Knotting Song" (Purcell), Miss Mildred Bowles. Miss Starkey, Miss Paul, and Mr George Paul caused considerable amusement playing the *role* of costermongers, with donkey and cart and wares complete, and they did a roaring trade throughout the afternoon. Mrs. Waldron had charge of a fruit stall, where cooling drinks could be obtained, and Miss Blunt had an attractive stall of coloured sketches. Miss Dodgson, of Woodstock, with Miss North and others had a fancy stall. Miss Bowen did great business telling fortunes under one of the large trees, and Miss Abbis and Miss Fletcher had a perfume smelling competition close by.

From four o'clock onwards Mr. W.C. Hurley, of Swacliffe, organised a novel balloon competition. For a shilling the patrons could send up a balloon, with a chance of winning a prize ranging from £1 downwards. Attached to each balloon was a label bearing the number of the competitor and a stamped address for it to be returned to Mr Hurley; the one coming from the longest distance winning the first prize, and a special prize is to be awarded any competitor whose balloon is returned from abroad. From four o'clock dainty teas were served by a number of young ladies, ably led by Mrs. Thorne and Miss Morrell, Mrs. T.H. Curtis and Mrs.

THE COTEFIELD FETE

Johnson, of Banbury, giving valuable assistance. Ingeborg Sogaard (Miss Grace Hoskyns), the celebrated dancer from the London Pavilion, gave some charming dances, as follows: "Solveig's Lied" (Grieg), Prelude op.28. No. 7 (Chopin), "Lied Sea Pieces" (E.McDowall). A novel side attraction was a treasure hunt in the kitchen garden, and last but not least, of the many side shows was a baby competition at the lodge for prizes given by Lady Leigh Hoskyns, the Hon. Mrs. Albert Brassey and the Hon. Mrs. Molyneux. The judges were Dr. Penrose, Miss Halstead (matron of the Horton Infirmary), Mrs. Gibson, of Oversands, and Miss Simmonds, of Adderbury, who made the following awards: - Children from one to two years 1. Bernard Baughn, 2. Ruby Jones. Children six to twelve months – 1. Willie Faulkner, 2. Marian Manning. There was a competition for dogs, Mr. Frank Butler, of Banbury, being the prize winner with a rough-haired fox terrier. In the early evening there were children's sports, followed by sports later in the evening for adults.

At six o'clock there was another concert in the hall, when a really attractive programme was performed, the following being the items: - "Bredon Hill" (George Butterworth), "Pleading" (Elgar), "Where my Caravan has rested" (Hermann Löhr), Miss Mildred Bowles: pianoforte solo, Mrs. Slater Harrison; "The Letter" (Sullivan), "Where be going?" (Somervell), "An Episode" and "If all the young maidens" (Hermann Löhr), "The Admiral's Yarn" (Paul Rubens), General Bowles: "Birds in the High Hall Garden" and "Go not, Happy Day" (Somervell), Miss Mildred Bowles. In the evening there was dancing on the lawn, the music being supplied by the Tadmarton Band, who had discoursed music throughout the day, and amongst the later attractions were an amusing fancy dress competition, and another dancing performance by Ingeborg Sogaard. The grounds were illuminated at night by Mr. T.H. Waters, of Banbury, who had carried out a very effective design of vari-coloured lights. The weather throughout was fine, and the threatening rain did not appear, so that the pleasures of the fete were enjoyed till a late hour, and it is sure to turn out a financial success, so whole-heartedly did the ladies and gentlemen concerned throw themselves into the arrangements.

THE FINE COMPANION

On 6 August, despite the outbreak of war, the *Banbury Guardian* still found space to print a short   notice about the results of the fête, and an apology for what was (when one looks at the advertisement) an understandable mistake:

THE COTEFIELD FETE IN AID OF THE HORTON INFIRMARY

We are asked to state that the Girls' Diocesan Association wish to thank all who contributed to the great success secured by this fete last week. We understand that the net result is expected to be about £100. We regret that the name of Miss Grace Hoskyns was, by an accident, given last week as being Ingeborg Sogaard, the clever exponent of dancing. Miss Grace Hoskyns was unable to fulfil her part in the programme owing to the death of Sir Chandos Hoskyns. Mr Hurley asks us to state that the results of the balloon competition will be announced next week. The balloon that has so far been returned from the furthest distance is from Builth Wells, Breconshire

By 13 August no one was interested any longer in the results of the balloon race: all attention was fixed across the Channel and not in the direction of Builth Wells and the west.

APPENDIX C

THE FOUNDATION AND EARLY YEARS OF THE ENGLISH FOLK DANCE SOCIETY

THE English Folk Dance Society, founded on 6 December 1911, grew out of the revival of interest in folk music which sprang up at the end of the 19th century all over Europe. Although in England many people were involved in the revival, the paramount name is Cecil James Sharp (1859-1924), who was not only a collector of folk song and dance but also a supreme populariser of both.

Sharp was born in London, read mathematics at Cambridge, worked in Australia in a bank and then as associate to the Chief Justice of South Australia. Despite his lack of formal training he then decided to follow his principal love, music, and managed to make his way by teaching and conducting. The formative experience of his life happened on 26 December 1899, when, staying at Headington near Oxford, he encountered a morris side who had come out to dance (albeit at the wrong time of year – it should have been Whitsun) in order to make a little money in a poor season. The concertina-player was William Kimber the younger, from whom Sharp noted his first five tunes. This awoke his interest in folk music, and gradually he began to collect songs himself. The Folk-Song Society had been founded in 1898, but was floundering for lack of funds, and it was Sharp's enthusiasm which brought about public interest. His *Folk-Songs from Somerset* appeared in five volumes between 1904 and 1909, *Songs of the West* (for which he edited the music) in 1905, and *English Folk-Songs for Schools* (in collaboration with Sabine Baring-Gould) in 1906.

In 1905, when Sharp was still chiefly concerned with folk songs, he was approached by Miss Mary Neal, organiser of the Espérance Working Girls' Club in Cumberland Market, St Pancras, who wanted to introduce her girls to folk songs. In a very short time

THE FINE COMPANION

Sharp's recommendations were so successful that Mary Neal wanted to add dancing, and this time Sharp suggested that she go to William Kimber. Kimber and a cousin came to London to teach the Espérance girls, who after only two evenings were able to give a performance of morris dancing (with folk songs and singing games) at their Christmas party. The programme was repeated in April 1906 at a public concert, Sharp giving the introductory lecture, and there was an immediate demand for intruction and performances. In 1907 Sharp collaborated with Herbert MacIlwaine, the Espérance musical director, in the publication of *The Morris Book*, part I, which was dedicated to 'our friends and pupils, the members of the Espérance Girls' Club'.

Gradually, however, Sharp became dissatisfied with the style of the Espérance girls' dancing, and went back to Kimber and other traditional performers to note the dances again; the revised versions came out in a second edition of *The Morris Book*. He was not happy with the standards of the Espérance Club, and when, late in 1907, Mary Neal came up with a plan for a society to develop and practice folk music Sharp was only marginally involved, and soon backed out; he was not part of the 'Association for the Revival and Practice of Folk Music' which was founded in 1908 with Mary Neal as Honorary Secretary. A working relationship still existed, however, and when in May 1909 folk song and dance competitions were held at Stratford-on-Avon, Sharp judged the singing and was a member of the panel (including Mary Neal) which judged the dancing.

Meanwhile the teaching of morris and country dancing in schools, had been sanctioned by the Board of Education, and there was a demand for trained teachers. Classes were arranged at the South-Western (later the Chelsea) Polytechnic, under Sharp's aegis; the Head Mistress of the Chelsea College, Miss Dorette Wilkie, was in sympathy with Sharp and allowed him a free hand. He taught students and staff, assisted on occasion by William Kimber, and there must have been other teachers, for when Helen Kennedy North later wrote of her memories of coming to 'Morris Dancing' she recorded attending without enthusiasm a short course in the academic year of 1907-8 and only in the following year encountering Cecil Sharp as a teacher.[1]

THE EARLY YEARS OF THE EFDS

In the summer term of 1907, 37 women attended an evening morris class, that is, not as part of the full-time Physical Education course.[2] In the following academic year, 1907-8, 168 women (some of them the same as the earlier class) took one or more of the evening morris classes.[3] Most of them were teachers but a few were apparently middle-class young ladies doing it for the fun of the thing. A formal School of Morris was set up there in 1909, by which time Sharp had a trained body of teachers available.

By the academic year 1910-11 the classes had multiplied to cover several levels of competence, the most prestigious of all being the Tuesday evening class from 8-9, the 'experimental', where dancers of tested competence tried out Sharp's latest discoveries. Among these dancers were the Karpeles sisters, who had been instant converts to folk-dancing after seeing the 1909 Stratford festival, Helen Kennedy North ('Madam'), and Daisy Daking.

Helen Kennedy (later Helen Kennedy North), as already mentioned, originally trained at Chelsea as a gym teacher and encountered morris as part of her course. She taught P.T. at Tunbridge Wells High School for only two terms before returning to London to be one of Sharp's teachers, presumably at Chelsea. She brought in her brother Douglas, later to be Sharp's successor as Director of the EFDS; he married Helen Karpeles. This Helen and her sister Maud enrolled at Chelsea in the autumn of 1909, and took up dancing with such enthusiasm that they soon organized a private group for practice at home. In April 1910 this group became a Folk-Dance Club and began to give very successful performances, both private and public, as well as classes.

This was the organization which in December 1911 turned into the English Folk-Dance Society. By then a 'proper' men's morris side was coming into being, several of whom (including the composer George Butterworth) attended the 'experimental' Chelsea class. They, with a team of women (including the Karpeles sisters but not Daisy Daking), habitually illustrated Sharp's lectures and demonstrations, joyfully giving up nearly every weekend from the inception of the Society until the outbreak of war in August 1914.

Following the Folk Festival at Stratford in the summer of 1909, in 1910 the governors of the Shakespeare Memorial Theatre invited the Espérance Guild to hold a summer school there in

THE FINE COMPANION

conjunction with the Shakespeare Festival, with the hope that this would become an annual event. With the growth of controversy between Mary Neal and Cecil Sharp the future organisation of the summer school fell into dispute, but in June 1911 responsibility was handed to Sharp. After the foundation of the EFDS in December 1911 the Stratford festival became their summer vacation school, and was held for four weeks each August until 1914. A one-week school was held at Chelsea after Christmas. This was resumed after the First War, but the summer school then moved to Cheltenham, and later to Aldeburgh.

1. Helen Kennedy North, 'Prelude, in *A Jubilee Symposium,* Folk-Music Journal, 1971.
2. King's College London archives, Chelsea College Fees Book, Evening Classes 1906-8, CA/SFB/25
3. King's College London archives, Chelsea College Fees Book, Day College for Women 1906-8, CA/SFB/10

APPENDIX D

EARLY REVIVAL FOLK-DANCING IN OXFORD

FOLK-DANCING in Oxford, in terms of the folk-dance revival, ante-dated the foundation of the EFDS itself and its Oxford branch by some four years. The Oxford Society for the Revival of the Folk-Dance, an off-shoot of Mary Neal's Association for the Revival and Practice of Folk Music (founded in April 1908), was formed in the summer of 1908.[1] A small committee, which included Charlotte Sidgwick, engaged a teacher to come down from London 'to instruct all who wish to learn in the method of dancing', and an inaugural meeting under the auspices of the Teachers' Guild was held on 10 October, with an address from Mary Neal and a demonstration by Iffley school-children. Their teacher, who presumably continued in Oxford for some time, was Rosina Mallet, one of the girls from Mary Neal's Espérance club, who is described as 'an East London club girl, looking about fourteen, almost a slum girl, probably a gypsy, a brown-eyed goblin with feet trained by London barrel organs'.[2] She was in fact nineteen, born in a working-class family in St Pancras in 1889; she married John Wilmhurst in 1913 and disappears from records; she and her husband may have emigrated, as other Espérance girls did.

The Espérance-related phase of folk-dancing in Oxford appears to have lasted until at least 1910. The Espérance Club itself gave a concert in the garden of Black Hall in St Giles on 26 June 1909, and in November 1911 Mary Neal mentioned that children of the 'Espérance Guild of Morris Dancers' (the successor of The Association for the Revival and Practice of Folk Music) had been invited to join a revived Headington side in a display in Oxford the previous year, that is, 1910, it seems reasonable to assume that these were local children.[3]

In the growing conflict between Cecil Sharp and Mary Neal it is clear that Oxford sided with Sharp, and when, in February

THE FINE COMPANION

1911, Sharp gave a lecture in Oxford on 'English Sword Dances', the demonstrators came from the Chelsea Physical Training College. In the following year folk-dance classes were advertised as arranged for the autumn, to be taught by 'a lady, highly trained at the Physical Training College, Chelsea'; this was Peggy Walsh, later Kettlewell, who went on to become the first secretary of the EFDS. DCD succeeded her in early 1912.

Although the Oxford branch of the EFDS was officially founded on 1 May 1912, this date was purely symbolic, the inaugural meeting in fact being held on 15 March. It amalgamated with the Oxford Folk Music Society, which had been formed in 1910, and presumably (though this is never explicitly mentioned) included a good number of those who had previously been involved with the Espérance group. At the March meeting various groups of children demonstrated dancing and singing games, and DCD's pupils from the Oxford Teachers' Club were advanced enough to demonstrate *My Lady Cullen* and *Newcastle* .

The University had by now taken up folk-dancing with enthusiasm. Marjorie Sidgwick tells us that 'a great man in the University took up dancing' (usually identified as Reg Tiddy, Fellow of Trinity, one of the notable dancers and certainly first chairman of the branch, but possibly more likely W. Hamilton Fyfe*, Fellow of Merton,), and 'a lady from Somerville' (Marjorie Taylor) became secretary of the society.[4]

In June 1912 the Oxford branch put on a demonstration in Thame; photographs in T*he Oxford Journal* (see Illustration 2) show the ladies (including DCD) wearing sunbonnets, plaits and aprons in the Espérance tradition rather than the more austere style later favoured by the EFDS.[5]

By February 1913 enough men had taken up morris to be able to supply a team to take part in the OUDS production of *The Shoemaker's Holiday*; this performance by 'the Dancing Dons' made a considerable stir, including as it did the Senior Proctor of the day – William Hamilton Fyfe*.

In the following April the branch put on a programme (arranged by DCD and Reg Tiddy) in All Souls' Library for the International Historical Congress, and in May provided a performance for Somerville College's 'At Home' to the workmen on their new Maitland Building. Three days later a newly discovered dance, *Christchurch Bells*, with other dances, was demonstrated at St Hilda's by children from two local schools, presumably taught by their teachers.

Moving out of Oxford itself, though still in an academic ambience, DCD gave a week's training in Morris to students at the Dorchester Missionary Training College (competent enough by the summer to provide demonstrators for an Extension Summer School, the University members not being available) and, probably at the same period, taught in the Elementary Girls' School in Dorchester, where 'two young teachers had been steadily practising on the children a few early Morris dances, gained by them from Miss Walsh so long ago as the autumn of 1911. Playford was welcomed as an entire novelty in the School'.[6]

With a party for Ruskin College on Whit Monday, a demonstration at a garden-party at Corpus in June, and an end-of-term general dance on 14 June in the High School grounds (the University Morris team demonstrating the Flamborough Sword Dance midway), not to mention private parties and a water-picnic up the Cherwell[6], the Oxford branch in 1913 was clearly going full steam ahead.

In 1914 the total membership of the Oxford branch was 124; DCD had 'about 100 pupils' for her class. On 12 February the branch enjoyed a lecture from Sir Francis Darwin, 'who studies Pipes and Tabors', and who explained 'showing both by his own instrumental performance and by lantern-pictures, how reed-music grew. One of his pipes he had cut for himself from a living stem of angelica ... It was a rare occasion. The newly-gathered native tunes, which he had by ear, must have inspired our University Team, for it danced notably even for itself. Mr Kimber was there with his concertina, and danced also ...' The term ended with a 'Playford Dance' in the Corn Exchange, centring on a demonstration but also with 'easy' dances 'longways for as many as will.'[6]

Meanwhile DCD had been almost overwhelmed by the demand for classes, not just in the university (where a dozen classes were held weekly) but in the schools and clubs and in the county.[7] Four assistants, including G.M. Girdlestone, were asked to help her. Lois Vidal started a class on Boar's Hill. As early as March 1912 more than eighty teachers belonging to the Oxford Teachers' Club were being taught by DCD, and several schools (in the poorest parts of the city) were already dancing. It is not clear whether the teachers' classes were subsumed into the EFDS classes, but it seems unlikely that the overall numbers had dropped by the summer of 1914.

Much of this activity ceased on the outbreak of war. Many of the university members joined up, or were too busy for dancing, and so folk-dancing in Oxford fell back to centring on the girls' clubs. On the other hand, the new Folk Music sub-committee seems to have been very active (presumably under Charlotte Sidgwick's leadership) and had success in November with a 'smoking concert' for about 300 men.

All the activity related above was emphatically 'town' or 'gown'; none of it had anything to do with the original folk dance of Oxfordshire, an area rich in morris tradition. Headington, now an Oxford suburb but then still separate from the city, was the home of William Kimber and was where Cecil Sharp saw his first morris. Bampton, in the west of the county, had its own morris tradition, as did (and does) Abingdon, then in the historic county of Berkshire but now in Oxfordshire and only eight miles from Oxford. But there is no indication that the eager members of the EFDS made any attempt to join or revive any of the traditional groups – perhaps they would not have been welcomed.

Nor is there apparently any record of what the 'old' morris men thought of it all. Only William Kimber the younger is recorded as linking the past with the new revival.

1. Leaflet issued by 'The Oxford Society for the Revival of Folk-Dance', quoted in Roy Judge, *The Ancient Men: the OUMM and its Background.*
2. Marjorie Sidgwick, *E.F.D.S. News* no.22, 1930
3. .Roy Judge, *op.cit.*
4. This may have been the earlier 'Society for the Revival of Folk-Dance', as Charlotte Sidgwick was the first secretary of the EFDS branch and had served 2 ½ years when she resigned in late 1914; Marjorie Taylor certainly succeeded her in that capacity, so there may have been some confusion over who did what when.

5. *The Oxford Journal* 12 June 1912, p.8.
6. Annual report for the Oxford branch, quoted in Judge, *op.cit.*
7. In 1914 Kidlington was a 'very completely articulated centre', and classes were recorded at Tackley, Yarnton, Steeple Aston, Burford, Reading, the Sibfords, Leafield, Ascott-under-Wychwood and Kelmscott.

BIBLIOGRAPHY

Boyes, Georgina (ed.), *Step Change: New Views on Traditional Dance*, Francis Boutle Publishers, London, 2001

Boyes, Georgina, *The Imagined Village: Culture, ideology and the English Folk Revival,* Manchester University Press, 1993; No Masters Co-operative Ltd, Leeds, 2010

Daking, D.C., *Feed My Sheep*, The Oxford Press, Anglo-Eastern Publishing Co. Ltd., 15 Cecil Court, Charing Cross Road, London, WC2, 1932

Daking, D.C., *Jungian Psychology and Modern Spiritual Thought* Anglo-Eastern Publishing Co. Ltd., London, 1933

Godfrey, Monica, *Elsie Jeanette Oxenham and Her Books*, Autolycus Publications, London, 1979

Godfrey, Monica, *The World of Elsie Jeanette Oxenham and her Books*, Girls Gone By, Coleford, 2003

Hepburne-Scott, Alexander Noel, *Letters to his mother and a few others*, privately printed, 1919

Judge, Roy, revised Hall, Ian, and Robinson, Gerard, *The Ancient Men, The OUMM [Oxford University Morris Men] and its Background,* 1970 and 1973, revision 1993. http://www.yetaco.plus.com/am39/oummhist.pdf

Karpeles, Maud, *Cecil Sharp, His Life and Work,* Routledge & Kegan Paul, London, 1967

Oxenham, Elsie Jeanette, *The Abbey Girls Again,* Collins, London, 1924

Oxenham, Elsie Jeanette, *The Abbey Girls Go Back to School,* Collins, London, 1922

Oxenham, Elsie Jeanette, *The Abbey Girls in Town,* Collins, London, 1925

Oxenham, Elsie Jeanette, *Jen of the Abbey School*, Collins, London, 1927, based on short stories published in Collins' *School girls' Annual* in 1923 (*The Girls of Rocklands School*), 1924, (*Jen's Presents*) and 1925 (*Treasures from the Snow*).

THE FINE COMPANION

For the complex publishing history of this book see the Girls
Gone By edition (2007) .

Oxenham, Elsie Jeanette, *The New Abbey Girls,*Collins, London,
1923

Oxenham, Elsie Jeanette, *Queen of the Abbey Girls,* Collins,
London, 1926

Vidal, Lois, *Magpie: The Autobiography of a Nymph Errant*
Little, Brown and Company, Boston, 1934

Watson, W.H.L., *Adventures of a Despatch Rider,* Blackwood,
London & Edinburgh, 1915

English Folk Dance Society Journal, 1914-1915
English Folk Dance Society News, 1921-1942
English Dance & Song, 1936

Oxford Dictionary of National Biography articles on

Butterworth, George Sainton Kaye
Buxton, Sir Thomas Fowell, 3rd Baronet
Buxton, Lady Victoria
Buxton, Noel Edward Noel-
Fyfe, William Hamilton
Karpeles, Maud Pauline
Kennedy, Douglas Neil
Kimber, William
Neal, Mary Sophia
Noel, Conrad Roden
Sharp, Cecil James
Sidgwick, Arthur
Sidgwick, Rose
Tiddy, Reginald John Elliott
Vidal, Mary Theresa